A Practical Book of Cornish Verbs

Compiled and edited by
Delia Brotherton

Published by Agan Tavas

ISBN 13: 978-1-901409-14-7
ISBN 10: 1-901409-14-7

Printed by Lulu

CONTENTS

FOREWORD by Ray Chubb / *RAGLAVAR gans Ray Chubb*

For some time, students of Unified Cornish have asked when we can have a comprehensive book of Cornish verbs. There are of course tables of verbs in dictionaries and text books for Unified but not every Cornish verb has been shown in a full table.

This book attempts to redress the balance. Although it is not as comprehensive as other compilations it uses references from Cornish historical texts which show quite clearly a strong tendency towards the use of the auxiliary verbs with the infinitive of the principal verb, rather than an unattested fully conjugated form of every verb. Even so, this book does include many fully conjugated verbs which have passed into everyday speech in Cornish even if they do not appear in historical literary works. In addition, the use of verb conjugations, other than auxiliary verbs, is often essential in order to write good verse.

Although it is not intended to be a comprehensive grammar book it will sit alongside other reference books and dictionaries and, hopefully, will be a welcome addition for the growing number of students who wish to further enrich their study of the Cornish language.

INTRODUCTION by Delia Brotherton / *COMENDYANS gans Delia Brotherton*

Students of *Kernewek*, in fact students of any subject, are always on the lookout for books which will help them expand their knowledge. As far as the Cornish language is concerned grammar books in general and verb listings in particular are not easy to find so the idea for "A Practical Book of Cornish Verbs" was born out of a desire to draw together all the information we could find scattered throughout various reference books, course notes, personal notes and scribblings.

The major sources of reference were the Morton Nance Memorial edition dictionary and Hilary Shaw's course notes, without which we would have struggled to find comprehensive and trustworthy references. Compilation of the book was helped enormously by the invaluable assistance of Pat Parry, who created the grid layout and input a sizeable chunk of the data, Clive Baker for lists of verbal nouns and constructions from adjectives, and Ray Chubb who spent hours on his computer double checking all the copy. Thank you all.

We hope you will find this book useful and time saving, especially on those occasions when you just can't quite remember those tricky little verb endings - we all know that feeling. Most of all we hope this book helps you get more enjoyment out of your study of *Kernewek.*

Oll an gwella.

THE BASICS OF VERB CONSTRUCTION

Verbs are made up of two parts,

- the STEM or ROOT which gives a general meaning, and
- the ENDINGS which give the tense and specific meaning of the verb

Some verbs are very regular, like ***PRENA***,
and some are very irregular, like ***BOS*** and ***Y'M BUS***.
Traditional Cornish tends to make more use of the auxiliary verbs -
GUL, MYNNES, GALLOS - with the infinitive of the principal verb in a sentence,

e.g	*my a wra y brena*	- I shall buy it
	ef a vyn aga gweles	- he will see them
	ny a yl y wul	- we can do it

VERB TENSES

PRESENT-FUTURE **I buy, I shall buy**
(unrestricted, indefinite time or duration in the present or expressing a desire to an action in the future)

IMPERFECT 1 **I was buying**
(simple past, action of undefined duration)

IMPERFECT 2 **I used to buy**
(habitual & continuous action done in the past, "the future in the past")

PRETERITE **I bought**
(an action done and completed at some time in the past)

PLUPERFECT **I had bought**
(an action already completed from some time in the past, use CONDITIONAL + particle *re*)

PRESENT PERFECT **I have bought**
(an action completed in the present time, no negative or direct interrogative form, use PRETERITE + particle *re* excluding *MOS* and *DOS* which have their own form of the Present Perfect*)*

FUTURE **I will buy**
(an action intended to be done in the future)

CONDITIONAL **I would buy**
(an action dependent on an unreal condition, something that is only imagined, the "if" situation)

PRESENT SUBJUNCTIVE **I may buy**
(an action that may happen in the present or future but doubt or uncertainty is implied)

IMPERFECT SUBJUNCTIVE **I might buy**
(an action that might happen, but doubt or uncertainty is implied)

IMPERATIVE **Buy!**
(a command given in most persons except 1st person singular)

PASSIVE or **IMPERSONAL** **One buys**
(draws attention to the person or thing acted upon rather than that doing the action)

PRESENT PARTICIPLE **Buying**
(an ongoing or continuous action being done, used with the long form of *BOS*)

PAST PARTICIPLE **Bought**
(a past action done, used with the short form of *BOS)*

ABBREVIATIONS USED IN THE VERB TABLES

S 1 – 1st person singular

S 2 – 2nd person singular

S 3 – 3rd person singular

S 3 M - 3rd person singular masculine (see ***y'm bus***)

S 3 F - 3rd person singular feminine (see ***y'm bus***)

P 1 – 1st person plural

P 2 – 2nd person plural

P 3 – 3rd person plural

0 - Passive voice – "one"

PARADIGM OF A REGULAR VERB

The box below gives the paradigm of a regular verb *PRENA*, showing the INFINITIVE (or VERBAL NOUN) followed by the STEM or ROOT of the verb (in brackets): followed by the meaning of the verb infinitive.

PRENA (PREN): to buy, redeem, pay for, merit				
	Present	**Imperfect**	**Preterite**	**Pluperfect**
S 1	prenaf	prenen	prenys	prensen
S 2	prenyth	prenes	prensys	prenses
S 3	pren	prena	prenas	prensa
P 1	prenyn	prenen	prensyn	prensen
P 2	prenough	preneugh	prensough	prenseugh
P 3	prenons	prenens	prensons	prensens
0	prenyr	prenys	prenas	prensys
	Present Subjunctive	**Imperfect Subjunctive**	**Imperative**	**Present Participle**
S 1	prennyf	prennen		ow prena
S 2	prenny	prennes	pren	
S 3	prenno	prenna	prenens	**Past Participle**
P 1	prennyn	prennen	prenyn	prenys
P 2	prennough	prenneugh	preneugh	
P 3	prennons	prennens	prenens	
0	prenner	prenys		

N.B. Usually used with *a* + 2nd state mutation and *orth*
In Future tense only 3rd person sing (S 3) is found: *prenvyth (my a brenvyth)*

Example: *why a'n prenvyth* - you shall pay for it; *y prenyr* - one buys

VERB ENDINGS:

	Present	**Imperfect**	**Preterite**	**Pluperfect**
S 1	-af	-en (-yn)	-ys	-sen
S 2	-yth	-es (-ys)	-sys	-ses
S 3	-	-a (-y)	-as	-sa
P 1	-yn	-en (-yn)	-syn	-sen
P 2	-ough	-eugh	-sough	-seugh
P 3	-ons	-ens	-sons	-sens
0	-yr, -er	-ys	-as, -ys	-sys
	Present Subjunctive	**Imperfect Subjunctive**		
S 1	-yf	-en		
S 2	-y	-es		
S 3	-o	-a		
P 1	-yn	-en		
P 2	-ough	-eugh		
P 3	-ons	-ens		
0	-er	-ys		

VERB LISTINGS

The listings begin with the auxiliary verbs (note ***y'm bus*** is not used as an auxiliary verb) followed by the remainder of the list in alphabetical order.

BOS: to be, take place, exist				
	Present short form	**Present long form**	**Imperfect short form**	**Imperfect long form**
S 1	of	esof	en	esen
S 2	os	esos	es	eses
S 3	yu	yma, us, usy	o	esa
P 1	on	eson	en	esen
P 2	ough	esough	eugh	eseugh
P 3	yns	ymons, esons	ens	esens
0	or	eder	os	edes
	Habitual Imperf	**Preterite**	**Future**	**Pluperfect**
S 1	bedhen	buf, bef	bydhaf	byen
S 2	bedhes	bus, bes	bydhyth	byes
S 3	bedha	bu, be	byth	bya
P 1	bedhen	ben	bydhyn	byen
P 2	bedheugh	beugh	bydhough	byeugh
P 3	bedhens	bons	bydhons	byens
0	bedhes	bus, bes	bydher	byes
	Present Subjunctive	**Imperfect Subjunctive**	**Imperative**	**Present Participle**
S 1	byf	ben		ow pos, ow pones
S 2	by	bes	byth	
S 3	bo	be	bedhens	**Past Participle**
P 1	ben, bon	ben	bedhen	(compounds only)
P 2	beugh, bough	beugh	bedheugh	bedhys
P 3	bons	bens	bedhens	
0	boer	bes		

Y'M BUS: to have, get				
	Present	**Imperfect 1**	**Imperfect 2**	**Preterite**
S 1	y'm bus	y'm bo	y'm bedha	y'm bu, be
S 2	y'th us	y'th o	y'(-th-) fedha	y'(-th-) fu, fe
S 3M	y'n jeves	y'n jevo	y'n jevedha	y'n jeva
S 3F	y's teves	y's tevo	y's tevedha	y's teva
P 1	y'gan bus	y'gan (-n-) bo	y'gan (-n-) bedha	y'gan (-n-) bu, be
P 2	y'gas bus	y'gas (-s-) bo	y'gas (-s-) bedha	y'gas (-s-) bu, be
P 3	y's teves	y's tevo	y's tevedha	y's teva
	Future	**Pluperfect**	**Present Subjunctive**	**Imperfect Subjunctive**
S 1	y'm byth	y'm bya	y'm bo	y'm be
S 2	y'(-th-) fyth	y'(-th-) fya	y'(-th-) fo	y'(-th-) fe
S 3M	y'n jevyth	y'n jevya	y'n jeffo	y'n jefffa
S 3F	y's tevyth	y's tevya	y's teffo	y's teffa
P 1	y'gan (-n-) byth	y'gan (-n-) bya	y'gan (-n-) bo	y'gan (-n-) be
P 2	y'gas (-s-) byth	y'gas (-s-) bya	y'gas (-s-) bo	y'gas (-s-) be
P 3	y's tevyth	y's tevya	y's teffo	y's teffa

N.B. ***BOS*** *with infixed pronouns* ***Y'M BUS*** is never used as an auxiliary verb.
Used with particles *a, re, ny, na* and with a simple pronoun followed by *a* or *re*
Imperfect 1 is simple, Imperfect 2 is habitual and conditional
Example: *my a'm bus* - I have; *hy re's teva* - she has had

GUL: to do, make, cause				
	Present	**Imperfect**	**Preterite**	**Pluperfect**
S 1	gwraf (gwrama)	gwren	gwruk	gwrussen
S 2	gwreth (gwreta)	gwres	gwrussys	gwrusses
S 3	gwra	gwre	gwruk	gwrussa
P 1	gwren	gwren	gwrussyn	gwrussen
P 2	gwreugh	gwreugh	gwrussough	gwrusseugh
P 3	gwrons	gwrens	gwrussons	gwrussens
0	gwrer			
	Present Subjunctive	**Imperfect Subjunctive**	**Imperative**	**Present Participle**
S 1	gwryllyf	gwrellen		ow cul
S 2	gwrylly	gwrelles	gwra	
S 3	gwrello	gwrella	gwrens	**Past Participle**
P 1	gwryllyn	gwrellen	gwren	gwres, gwrys
P 2	gwrellough	gwrelleugh	gwreugh	
P 3	gwrellons	gwrellens	gwrens	

GALLOS (GYL): to be able, "can"				
	Present	**Imperfect**	**Preterite**	**Pluperfect**
S 1	gallaf	gyllyn	gyllys	galsen
S 2	gyllyth (gylta)	gyllys	gylsys	galses
S 3	gyl	gylly	gallas	galsa
P 1	gyllyn	gyllyn	gylsyn	galsen
P 2	gyllough	gylleugh	gylsough	galseugh
P 3	gyllons	gyllens	galsons	galsens
0	gyllyr	gyllys	gallas	galsys, galser
	Present Subjunctive	**Imperfect Subjunctive**	**Imperative**	**Participles**
S 1	gyllyf	gallen		
S 2	gylly	galles		
S 3	gallo	galla		
P 1	gyllyn	gallen		
P 2	gyllough	galleugh		
P 3	gallons	gallens		
0	galler	galles		

N.B. In Future tense only 3rd person sing (S 3) is found: *gylwyth (my a ylwyth)*

MYNNES (MYN): to want to, wish, be willing				
	Present	**Imperfect**	**Preterite**	**Pluperfect**
S 1	mynnaf	mynnen	mynnys	mynsen
S 2	mynnyth (mynta)	mynnes	mynsys	mynses (mynsta)
S 3	myn	mynna	mynnas	mynsa
P 1	mynnyn	mynnen	mynsyn	mynsen
P 2	mynnough	mynneugh	mynsough	mynseugh
P 3	mynnons	mynnens	mynsons	mynsens
0	mynnyr	mynnes	mynnas	mynsys
	Present Subjunctive	**Imperfect Subjunctive**	**Imperative**	**Present Participle**
S 1	mynnyf	mynnen		ow mynnes
S 2	mynny	mynnes		
S 3	mynno	mynna		**Past Participle**
P 1	mynnyn	mynnen		mynnys
P 2	mynnough	mynneugh		
P 3	mynnons	mynnens		
0	mynner	mynnes		

N.B. Used with *orth*

MOS: to go				
	Present	**Imperfect**	**Preterite**	**Pluperfect**
S 1	af	en	yth	gylsen
S 2	eth	es	ythys	gylses
S 3	a	e	eth	galsa
P 1	en	en	ethen	gylsen
P 2	eugh	eugh	etheugh	gylseugh
P 3	ons	ens	ethons	gylsens

	Present Subjunctive	**Imperfect Subjunctive**	**Perfect**	**Imperative**	**Present Participle**
S 1	yllyf	ellen	galsof		ow mos, ow mones
S 2	ylly	elles	galsos	ke, a	
S 3	ello	ella	gallas	ens	**Past Participle**
P 1	yllyn	ellen	galson	dun	gyllys, es
P 2	yllough	elleugh	galsough	keugh, eugh	
P 3	ellons	ellens	galsons	ens	

Example: *mos gans* - to be taken, won or gained by; *mos rag* - to vouch for

DOS: to come				
	Present	**Imperfect**	**Preterite**	**Pluperfect**
S 1	dof	den	duth	dothyen
S 2	duth	des	duthys	dothyes
S 3	de, du	do	deth	dothya
P 1	dun	den	duthen	dothyen
P 2	deugh	deugh	dutheugh	dothyeugh
P 3	dons	dens	duthons, dethons	dothyens
0	deer			

	Present Subjunctive	**Imperfect Subjunctive**	**Perfect**	**Imperative**	**Present Participle**
S 1	dyffyf	deffen	dufef		ow tos
S 2	dyffy	deffes	dufes	dus	
S 3	deffo	deffa	dufa, deva	dens	**Past Participle**
P 1	dyffyn	deffen	dufen	dun	devedhys
P 2	dyffough	deffeugh	dufeugh	deugh	
P 3	dyffons	deffens	dufons	dens	

Example: *dos gans* - to carry off; *dos ha* + infinitive - to come to, to happen to; *dos dre gans* - to pierce, run through with; *kens nos dos* - before night comes

AMMA (AM): to kiss				
	Present	**Imperfect**	**Preterite**	**Pluperfect**
S 3	am	ymmy	ammas	amsa
	Present Subjunctive	**Imperfect Subjunctive**	**Imperative**	**Present Participle**
S 3	ammo	amma		owth amma
				Past Participle
				ymmys

N.B. Usually used with *dhe* + 2nd state mutation.

ANKEVY (ANCOF): to forget				
	Present	**Imperfect**	**Preterite**	**Pluperfect**
S 3	ankef	ankevy	ancovas	ancofsa
	Present Subjunctive	**Imperfect Subjunctive**	**Imperative**	**Present Participle**
S 3	ancoffo	ancova		owth ankevy
				Past Participle
				ankevys

ANNYA (ANNY): to annoy, bother, tire				
	Present	**Imperfect**	**Preterite**	**Pluperfect**
S 3	anny	annya	annyas	annysa
	Present Subjunctive	**Imperfect Subjunctive**	**Imperative**	**Present Participle**
S 3	annyo	annya		owth annya
				Past Participle
				annyes

Example: *ny'th annyaf* - I will not trouble thee

ANWESY (ANWOS): to catch cold				
	Present	**Imperfect**	**Preterite**	**Pluperfect**
S 3	anwos	anwesy	anwosas	anwossa
	Present Subjunctive	**Imperfect Subjunctive**	**Imperative**	**Present Participle**
S 3	anwosso	anwosa		owth anwesy
				Past Participle
				anwesys

ASSENTYA (ASSENT): to agree, acquiesce				
	Present	**Imperfect**	**Preterite**	**Pluperfect**
S 3	assent	assentya	assentyas	assentsa
	Present Subjunctive	**Imperfect Subjunctive**	**Imperative**	**Present Participle**
S 3	assentyo	assentya		owth assentya
				Past Participle
				assentyes

Example: *assentya gans* - to take the side of

ASWON/ASWONVOS: to know, recognise, be acquainted with				
	Present	**Imperfect**	**Preterite**	**Pluperfect**
S 1			aswonfys	
S 3	aswon	aswony	aswonys	aswonsa
	Present Subjunctive	**Imperfect Subjunctive**	**Imperative**	**Present Participle**
S 3	aswonno	aswonna		owth aswon
				Past Participle
				aswonys

N.B. Usually used with *gans*

Verbs can be constructed from an adjective by adding the ***-he*** syllable as a suffix creating a verb meaning "to make or enable"
i.e. *BER* (short) + *HE* = *BERHE* : *to shorten*
All similar verbs follow the pattern for ***BERHE*** – there are more examples on page 107

BERHE (BERHA): to shorten, grow shorter				
	Present	**Imperfect**	**Preterite**	**Pluperfect**
S 1	berhaf	berhyn	berhys	berhasen
S 2	berhyth	berhys	berhasys	berhases
S 3	berha	berhy	berhas	berhasa
P 1	berhyn	berhyn	berhasyn	berhasen
P 2	berhough	berheugh	berhasough	berhaseugh
P 3	berhons	berhens	berhasons	berhasens
	Present Subjunctive	**Imperfect Subjunctive**	**Imperative**	**Present Participle**
S 1	berhahyf	berhahen		ow perhe
S 2	berhahy	berhahes	berha	
S 3	berhaho	berhaha	berhes, berhens	**Past Participle**
P 1	berhahyn	berhahen	berhen	berhes, berhys
P 2	berhahough	berhaheugh	berheugh	
P 3	berhahons	berhahens	berhens	

BEWA (BEW): to live				
	Present	**Imperfect**	**Preterite**	**Pluperfect**
S 3	bew	bewa	bewas	bewsa
	Present Subjunctive	**Imperfect Subjunctive**	**Imperative**	**Present Participle**
S 3	bewo	bewa		ow pewa
				Past Participle
				bewys

Example: *bewa orth* - to live upon something (by eating it)

BLASA (BLAS): to savour, relish				
	Present	**Imperfect**	**Preterite**	**Pluperfect**
S 3	blas	blasa	blasas	blassa
	Present Subjunctive	**Imperfect Subjunctive**	**Imperative**	**Present Participle**
S 3	blasso	blasa		ow plasa
				Past Participle
				blesys

BUDHY (BUTH): to drown, founder				
	Present	**Imperfect**	**Preterite**	**Pluperfect**
S 3	buth	budhy	budhys	buthsa
	Present Subjunctive	**Imperfect Subjunctive**	**Imperative**	**Present Participle**
S 3	butho	budha		ow pudhy
				Past Participle
				budhys

CABLY (CABEL): to blame, censure				
	Present	**Imperfect**	**Preterite**	**Pluperfect**
S 3	cabel	cably	cablas	cabelsa
	Present Subjunctive	**Imperfect Subjunctive**	**Imperative**	**Present Participle**
S 3	cabello	cabella		ow cably
				Past Participle
				cablys

CAFOS (CAF): to find, get, have, discover, invent				
	Present	**Imperfect**	**Preterite**	**Pluperfect**
S 1	cafaf	kefyn	kefys	cafsen
S 2	kefyth	kefys	kefsys	cafses
S 3	kyf	kefy	cafas	cafsa
P 1	kefyn	kefyn	kefsyn	cafsen
P 2	kefough	kefeugh	kefsough	cafseugh
P 3	kefons	kefens	cafsons	cafsens
	Present Subjunctive	**Imperfect Subjunctive**	**Imperative**	**Present Participle**
S 1	kyffyf	caffen		ow cafos
S 2	kyffy	caffes	caf	
S 3	caffo	caffa	kefens	**Past Participle**
P 1	kyffyn	caffen	kefyn	kefys
P 2	kyffough	caffeugh	kefeugh	
P 3	caffons	caffens	kefens	

N.B. Can be used with *dhe* + 2nd state mutation

CAMDYBY (CAMDYP): to err in thought				
	Present	**Imperfect**	**Preterite**	**Pluperfect**
S 3	camdyp	camdyby	camdybys	camdypsa
	Present Subjunctive	**Imperfect Subjunctive**	**Imperative**	**Present Participle**
S 3	camdyppo	camdyba		ow camdyby
				Past Participle
				camdybys

N.B. Used with *war* + 2nd state mutation
Example: *camdyby war* – to be mistaken

CAMPOLLA (CAMPOL): to mention				
	Present	**Imperfect**	**Preterite**	**Pluperfect**
S 3	campol	campolla	campollas	campolsa
	Present Subjunctive	**Imperfect Subjunctive**	**Imperative**	**Present Participle**
S 3	campollo	campolla		ow campolla
				Past Participle
				campollys

CAMPYA (CAMP): to camp				
	Present	**Imperfect**	**Preterite**	**Pluperfect**
S 3	camp	campya	campyas	campsa
	Present Subjunctive	**Imperfect Subjunctive**	**Imperative**	**Present Participle**
S 3	campyo	campya		ow campya
				Past Participle
				campyes

CANA (CAN): to sing				
	Present	**Imperfect**	**Preterite**	**Pluperfect**
S 3	can	cana	canas	cansa
	Present Subjunctive	**Imperfect Subjunctive**	**Imperative**	**Present Participle**
S 3	canno	canna	can	ow cana
				Past Participle
				kenys

CARA (CAR): to love, like, care for				
	Present	**Imperfect**	**Preterite**	**Pluperfect**
S 1	caraf	caren	kerys	carsen
S 2	keryth	cares	kersys	carses
S 3	car	cara	caras	carsa
P 1	keryn	caren	kersyn	carsen
P 2	kerough	careugh	kersough	carseugh
P 3	carons	carens	carsons	carsens
	Present Subjunctive	**Imperfect Subjunctive**	**Imperative**	**Present Participle**
S 1	kyrryf	carren		ow cara
S 2	kyrry	carres	car	
S 3	carro	carra	carens	**Past Participle**
P 1	kyrryn	carren	keryn	kerys
P 2	kyrrough	carreugh	kereugh	
P 3	carrons	carrens	carens	

N.B. In Future tense only 3rd person sing (S 3) is found: *carvyth* (*my a garvyth)*
Example: *yn un gara* - loving, lovingly; *caradow* - beloved, lovable

CHANJYA (CHANJ): to change, alter				
	Present	**Imperfect**	**Preterite**	**Pluperfect**
S 3	chanj	chanjya	chanjyas	chanchsa
	Present Subjunctive	**Imperfect Subjunctive**	**Imperative**	**Present Participle**
S 3	chanjyo	chanjya		ow chanjya
				Past Participle
				chanjyes

CHERSYA (CHERS): to cherish, caress, fondle				
	Present	**Imperfect**	**Preterite**	**Pluperfect**
S 3	chers	chersya	chersyas	cherssa
	Present Subjunctive	**Imperfect Subjunctive**	**Imperative**	**Present Participle**
S 3	cherssyo	chersya		ow chersya
				Past Participle
				chersyes

CLEWES (CLEW)*/ CLOWAS (CLOW): to hear, feel, smell				
	Present	**Imperfect**	**Preterite**	**Pluperfect**
S 1	clewaf/clowaf	clewen/clowen	clewys/clowys	clewsen/clowsen
S 2	clewyth/clowyth	clewes/clowes	clewsys/clowsys	clewses/clowses
S 3	clew/clow	clewo/clowo	clewas/clowas	clewsa/clowsa
P 1	clewyn/clowyn	clewen/clowen	clewsyn/clowsyn	clewsen/clowsen
P 2	clewough/ clowough	clewyeugh/ cloweugh	clewsough/ clowsough	clewseugh/ clowseugh
P 3	clewons/clowons	clewens/clowens	clewsons/clowsons	clewsens/clowsens
0	clewyr	clewes	clewas	clewsys
	Present Subjunctive	**Imperfect Subjunctive**	**Imperative**	**Present Participle**
S 1	clewfyf/clowfyf	clewfen/clowfen		ow clewes/ ow clowas
S 2	clewfy/clowfy	clewfes/clowfes	clew/clow	
S 3	clewfo/clowfo	clewfe/clowfe	clewens/clowens	**Past Participle**
P 1	clewfen/clowfen	clewfen/clowfen	clewyn/clowyn	clewys/clowys
P 2	clewfeugh/ clowfeugh	clewfeugh/ clowfeugh	clewyeugh/ clowyeugh	
P 3	clewfons/clowfons	clewfens/clowfens	clewens/clowens	

*Use *clew* or *clow* as a stem - (*clow* is later Cornish)
N.B. In Future tense only 3rd person sing (S 3)is found: *clewvyth (my a glewvyth).* Used with *gans* or *a* + 2nd state mutation

CODHA (COTH): to fall				
	Present	**Imperfect**	**Preterite**	**Pluperfect**
S 3	coth	codha	codhas	cothsa
	Present Subjunctive	**Imperfect Subjunctive**	**Imperative**	**Present Participle**
S 3	cotho	cotha		ow codha
				Past Participle
				codhys

Example: *codha war, worth* - to befall to; *gasa dhe godha* - to let fall, drop

COLA (COL): to trust, believe, lend an ear				
	Present	**Imperfect**	**Preterite**	**Pluperfect**
S 3	col	cola	colas	colsa
	Present Subjunctive	**Imperfect Subjunctive**	**Imperative**	**Present Participle**
S 3	collo	colla		ow cola
				Past Participle
				colys

N.B. Usually used with *orth*

COMENDYA (COMEND): to entrust, commend				
	Present	**Imperfect**	**Preterite**	**Pluperfect**
S 3	comend	comendya	comendyas	comentsa
	Present Subjunctive	**Imperfect Subjunctive**	**Imperative**	**Present Participle**
S 3	comendyo	comendya		ow comendya
				Past Participle
				comendyes

CONVEDHES (CONVETH): to understand				
	Present	**Imperfect**	**Preterite**	**Pluperfect**
S 3	conveth	convedhy	convedhas	convedhas
	Present Subjunctive	**Imperfect Subjunctive**	**Imperative**	**Present Participle**
S 3	convetho	convedha		ow convedhes
				Past Participle
				convedhys

COSTYA (COST): to cost				
	Present	**Imperfect**	**Preterite**	**Pluperfect**
S 3	cost	costya	costyas	costsa
	Present Subjunctive	**Imperfect Subjunctive**	**Imperative**	**Present Participle**
S 3	costyo	costya		ow costya
				Past Participle
				costyes

COWLWUL (COWLWRA): to finish completely				
	Present	**Imperfect**	**Preterite**	**Pluperfect**
S 3	cowlwra	cowlwre	cowlwruk	cowlwrussa
	Present Subjunctive	**Imperfect Subjunctive**	**Imperative**	**Present Participle**
S 3	cowlwrello	cowlwrella		ow cowlwul
				Past Participle
				cowlwres, cowlrys

CRAKKYA (CRAK): to break, snap, crack				
	Present	**Imperfect**	**Preterite**	**Pluperfect**
S 3	crak	crakkya	crakkyas	craksa
	Present Subjunctive	**Imperfect Subjunctive**	**Imperative**	**Present Participle**
S 3	crakkyo	crakkya		ow crakkya
				Past Participle
				crakkyes

CREGY (CROK): to hang				
	Present	**Imperfect**	**Preterite**	**Pluperfect**
S 3	crek	cregy	crogas	croksa
	Present Subjunctive	**Imperfect Subjunctive**	**Imperative**	**Present Participle**
S 2			crok	ow cregy
S 3	crokko	croga		
				Past Participle
				cregys

CRONKYA (CRONK): to beat				
	Present	**Imperfect**	**Preterite**	**Pluperfect**
S 3	cronk	cronkya	cronkyas	cronksa
	Present Subjunctive	**Imperfect Subjunctive**	**Imperative**	**Present Participle**
S 3	cronkyo	cronkya		ow cronkya
				Past Participle
				cronkyes

N.B. Usually used with *orth*

CRYA (CRY): to cry out				
	Present	**Imperfect**	**Preterite**	**Pluperfect**
S 3	cry	crya	cryas	crysa
	Present Subjunctive	**Imperfect Subjunctive**	**Imperative**	**Present Participle**
S 3	cryo	crya		ow crya
				Past Participle
				cryes

Example: *crya war* - to call to, call on

CRYSY (CRYS) / CRESY (CRES) / CREJY (CREJ): to believe				
	Present	**Imperfect**	**Preterite**	**Pluperfect**
S 1	crysaf/cresaf/crejaf	crysyn/cresyn/ crejyn	crysys/cresys/crejys	cryssen/cressen
S 2	crysyth/cresyth/ crejyth	crysys/cresys/ crejys	cryssys/cressys	crysses/cresses
S 3	crys/cres/crej	crysy/cresy/crejy	crysys/cresys/crejys	cryssa/cressa
P 1	crysyn/cresyn/ crejyn	crysyn/cresyn/ crejyn	cryssyn/cressyn	cryssen/cressen
P 2	crysough/cresough/ crejough	cryseugh/creseugh /crejeugh	cryssough/ cressough	crysseugh/ cresseugh
P 3	crysons/cresons/ crejons	crysens/cresens/ crejens	cryssons/cressons	cryssens/ cressens
0	crysyr/cresyr/crejyr	crysys/cresys/crejys	crysys/cresys/crejys	cryssys/cressys
	Present Subjunctive	**Imperfect Subjunctive**	**Imperative**	**Present Participle**
S 1	cryssyf/cressyf	cryssen/cressen		ow crysy/ow cresy/ow crejy
S 2	cryssy/cressy	crysses/cresses	crys/cres/crej	
S 3	crysso/cresso	cryssa/cressa	crysens/cresens/ crejens	
P 1	cryssyn/cressyn	cryssen/cressen	crysyn/cresyn/ crejyn	
P 2	crysseugh/ cresseugh	crysseugh/ cresseugh	cryseugh/creseugh/ crejeugh	
P 3	cryssons/cressons	cryssens/cressens	crysens/cresens/ crejens	**Past Participle**
0	cryser/cresyr	cryses/creses		crysys/cresys/ crejys

N.B. Used with *dhe* + 2nd state mutation
There are no references in texts to double j - *"jj"*
Example: *crysy dhym* - believe me; *crysy ynno* - believing in him

CUDHA (CUTH): to cover, hide				
	Present	**Imperfect**	**Preterite**	**Pluperfect**
S 3	cuth	cudha	cudhas	cuthsa
	Present Subjunctive	**Imperfect Subjunctive**	**Imperative**	**Present Participle**
S 3	cutho	cudha		ow cudha
				Past Participle
				cudhys

N.B. Used with *rak*

CUNTELL (CUNTELL): to gather				
	Present	**Imperfect**	**Preterite**	**Pluperfect**
S 3	cuntell	cuntellas	cuntelas	cuntelsa
	Present Subjunctive	**Imperfect Subjunctive**	**Imperative**	**Present Participle**
S 3	cuntello	cuntella		ow cuntell
				Past Participle
				cuntellys

CUSCA: (CUSK) to sleep, go mouldy				
	Present	**Imperfect**	**Preterite**	**Pluperfect**
S 3	cusk	cusca	cuscas	cussa
	Present Subjunctive	**Imperfect Subjunctive**	**Imperative**	**Present Participle**
S 2			cusk	ow cusca
S 3	cusco	cusca		
				Past Participle

Example: *cusca war dha dor* - to sleep face downwards

DALLETH (DALLATH): to begin				
	Present	**Imperfect**	**Preterite**	**Pluperfect**
S 3	dalleth	dallethy	dallathas	dallathsa
	Present Subjunctive	**Imperfect Subjunctive**	**Imperative**	**Present Participle**
S 3	dallatho	dallatha		ow talleth
				Past Participle
				dallethys

DANVON (DANVON): to send				
	Present	**Imperfect**	**Preterite**	**Pluperfect**
S 3	danvon	danveny	danvonas	danvonsa
	Present Subjunctive	**Imperfect Subjunctive**	**Imperative**	**Present Participle**
S 3	danvonno	danvonna		ow tanvon
				Past Participle
				danvenys

N.B. Usually used with *dhe* + 2nd state mutation
Example: *danvon warlergh* - to send for, send to fetch

DARBARY (DARBAR): to prepare, provide, equip, supply				
	Present	**Imperfect**	**Preterite**	**Pluperfect**
S 3	darbar	darbary	darbarys	darbarsa
	Present Subjunctive	**Imperfect Subjunctive**	**Imperative**	**Present Participle**
S 3	darbarro	darbarra		ow tarbary
				Past Participle
				darbarys

N.B. Usually used with *dhe* + 2nd state mutation.

DEGEA (DEGE): to shut				
	Present	**Imperfect**	**Preterite**	**Pluperfect**
S 3	dege	degea	degeas	degesa
	Present Subjunctive	**Imperfect Subjunctive**	**Imperative**	**Present Participle**
S 3	degesso	degessa		ow tegea
				Past Participle
				deges

DEGEMERES (DEGEMER): to receive, admit, seize				
	Present	**Imperfect**	**Preterite**	**Pluperfect**
S 3	degemer	degemery	degemeras	degemersa
	Present Subjunctive	**Imperfect Subjunctive**	**Imperative**	**Present Participle**
S 3	degemerro	degemerra		ow tegemeres
				Past Participle
				degemerys

DERYVAS (DERYF): to tell, declare, recount, state				
	Present	**Imperfect**	**Preterite**	**Pluperfect**
S 3	deryf	deryvy	deryvys	deryfsa
	Present Subjunctive	**Imperfect Subjunctive**	**Imperative**	**Present Participle**
S 2			deryf	ow teryvas
S 3	deryffo	deryffa		
				Past Participle
				deryvys

N.B. Usually used with *dhe* + 2nd state mutation, *orth*.

DESCRYFA (DESCRYF): to describe				
	Present	**Imperfect**	**Preterite**	**Pluperfect**
S 3	descryf	descryfa	descryfas	descryfsa
	Present Subjunctive	**Imperfect Subjunctive**	**Imperative**	**Present Participle**
S 3	descryfo	descryfa		ow tescryfa
				Past Participle
				descryfys

DESEVOS (DESEF): to presume				
	Present	**Imperfect**	**Preterite**	**Pluperfect**
S 3	desef	desevya	desevas	desefsa
	Present Subjunctive	**Imperfect Subjunctive**	**Imperative**	**Present Participle**
S 3	desseffo	deseva		ow tesevos
				Past Participle
				desevys

N.B. 1st person plural (P 1) Imperfect Subjunctive in the negative is *na dheseven* (*na thesan* in texts*)*.

DESMYGY (DESMYK): to guess				
	Present	**Imperfect**	**Preterite**	**Pluperfect**
S 3	desmyk	desmyga	desmygys	desmyksa
	Present Subjunctive	**Imperfect Subjunctive**	**Imperative**	**Present Participle**
S 3	desmycco	desmyga		ow tesmygy
				Past Participle
				desmygys

DEVERA (DEVER): to drip, trickle, pour, shower, shed, bleed				
	Present	**Imperfect**	**Preterite**	**Pluperfect**
S 3	dever	devera	deveras	deversa
	Present Subjunctive	**Imperfect Subjunctive**	**Imperative**	**Present Participle**
S 3	deverro	deverra		ow tevera
				Past Participle

DEWEDHA (DEWETH): to end, finish				
	Present	**Imperfect**	**Preterite**	**Pluperfect**
S 3	deweth	dewedha	dewedhys	dewethsa
	Present Subjunctive	**Imperfect Subjunctive**	**Imperative**	**Present Participle**
S 3	dewetho	dewetha		ow tewedha
				Past Participle
				dewedhys

DEWHELES (DEWHEL): to return				
	Present	**Imperfect**	**Preterite**	**Pluperfect**
S 3	dewhel	dewhely	dewhelys	dewhelsa
	Present Subjunctive	**Imperfect Subjunctive**	**Imperative**	**Present Participle**
S 3	dewhello	dewhella		ow tewheles
				Past Participle
				dewhelys

DEWYS (DEWYS): to choose				
	Present	**Imperfect**	**Preterite**	**Pluperfect**
S 3	dewys	dewysy	dewysys	dewyssa
	Present Subjunctive	**Imperfect Subjunctive**	**Imperative**	**Present Participle**
S 3	dewysso	dewyssa		ow tewys
				Past Participle
				dewysys

DOBLA (DOBEL): to double				
	Present	**Imperfect**	**Preterite**	**Pluperfect**
S 3	dobel	dobla	doblas	dobelsa
	Present Subjunctive	**Imperfect Subjunctive**	**Imperative**	**Present Participle**
S	dobello	dobella		ow tobla
				Past Participle
				doblys

DON (DOK)/DEGY : to carry, bear, bring, take, convey				
	Present	**Imperfect**	**Preterite**	**Pluperfect**
S 1	degaf	degyn	duk	deksen
S 2	degeth	degys	duges	dekses
S 3	dek	degy	duk	deksa
P 1	degon/degen	degyn	dugon	deksen
P 2	degough	degeugh	dugough	dekseugh
P 3	degons	degens	dugons	deksens
	Present Subjunctive	**Imperfect Subjunctive**	**Imperative**	**Past Participle**
S 1	dykkyf	dekken		ow ton / ow tegy
S 2	dykky	dekkes	dok	
S 3	decco	decca / dega	degens	**Past Participle**
P 1	dykkyn	dekken	degen	degys
P 2	dyccough	dekkeugh	degeugh	
P 3	doccons	dekkens	degens	

Example: *don dystyny* - to bear witness; *don gans* - to bring off, take with; *don dhyworth* - to take away from

DONSYA (DONS): to dance				
	Present	**Imperfect**	**Preterite**	**Pluperfect**
S 3	dons	donsya	donsyas	donsa
	Present Subjunctive	**Imperfect Subjunctive**	**Imperative**	**Present Participle**
S 3	donsyo	donsya		ow tonsya
				Past Participle
				donsyes

DREHEDHES (DREHETH): to attain, reach completely				
	Present	**Imperfect**	**Preterite**	**Pluperfect**
S 3	dreheth	drehedhy	drehedhas	drehethsa
	Present Subjunctive	**Imperfect Subjunctive**	**Imperative**	**Present Participle**
S 3	drehetho	drehetha		ow trehedhes
				Past Participle
				drehedhys

N.B. Can be used with *gans, ha*

DREHEVEL (DREHAF): to raise, build				
	Present	**Imperfect**	**Preterite**	**Pluperfect**
S 3	drehaf	drehevy	drehevys	drehafsa
	Present Subjunctive	**Imperfect Subjunctive**	**Imperative**	**Present Participle**
S 2			drehaf, drefa	ow trehevel
S 3	drehaffo	drehaffa		
				Past Participle
				drehevys

DRY (DORO): to bring, take with one, persuade				
	Present	**Imperfect**	**Preterite**	**Pluperfect**
S 1	drof	dren	dres	drosen
S 2	dreth	dres	dressys	droses
S 3	dora, dre	dry	dros	drosa
P 1	dren	dren	dresen	drosen
P 2	drough	dreugh	dresough	droseugh
P 3	drons	drens	dresons	drosens
	Present Subjunctive	**Imperfect Subjunctive**	**Imperative**	**Present Participle**
S 1	dryllyf	drollen		ow try
S 2	drylly	drolles	doro, doroy	
S 3	drollo	drolla	drens	**Past Participle**
P 1	dryllyn	drollen	dren	dres
P 2	dryllough	drolleugh	dreugh	
P 3	dryllons	drollens	drens	

Example: *dry yn mes* - to put out; *dry dhe/ dry yntra dywla* - to give up

DYBRY (DEBER): to eat, tickle				
	Present	**Imperfect**	**Preterite**	**Pluperfect**
S 1	debraf	dybryn	dybrys	depsen
S 2	dybryth	dybrys	dypsys	depses
S 3	deber	dybry	dybrys	depsa
P 1	dybryn	dybryn	dypsyn	depsen
P 2	debrough	debreugh	depsough	depseugh
P 3	debrons	debrens	depsons	depsens
	Present Subjunctive	**Imperfect Subjunctive**	**Imperative**	**Present Participle**
S 1	dybryf	debren		ow tybry
S 2	dybry	debres	deber	
S 3	deppro	debra	debrens	**Past Participle**
P 1	dybryn	debren	dybryn	dybrys
P 2	debrough	debreugh	debreugh	
P 3	depprons	debrens	debrens	

Example: *kens es dybry* - before knocking off work, without a break

DYESKYNNA (DYESKYN): to descend				
	Present	**Imperfect**	**Preterite**	**Pluperfect**
S 3	dyeskyn	dyeskynna	dyeskynnas	dyeskynsa
	Present Subjunctive	**Imperfect Subjunctive**	**Imperative**	**Present Participle**
S 3	dyeskynno	dyeskynna		ow tyeskynna
				Past Participle
				dyeskynnys

DYFEN (DYFEN): to prohibit				
	Present	**Imperfect**	**Preterite**	**Pluperfect**
S 3	dyfen	dyfeny	dyfenas	dyfensa
	Present Subjunctive	**Imperfect Subjunctive**	**Imperative**	**Present Participle**
S 3	dyfenno	dyfenna		ow tyfen
				Past Participle
				dyfennys

N.B. Used with *orth, na* + 2nd state and a subjunctive

DYFUNA (DYFUN): to wake up				
	Present	**Imperfect**	**Preterite**	**Pluperfect**
S 3	dyfun	dyfuna	dyfunas	dyfunsa
	Present Subjunctive	**Imperfect Subjunctive**	**Imperative**	**Present Participle**
S 3	dyfuno	dyfuna		ow tyfuna
				Past Participle
				dyfunys

DYGHTYA (DYGHT): to use, provide, serve, order				
	Present	**Imperfect**	**Preterite**	**Pluperfect**
S 3	dyght	dyghtya	dyghtyas	dyghtsa
	Present Subjunctive	**Imperfect Subjunctive**	**Imperative**	**Present Participle**
S 3	dyghtyo	dyghtya		ow tyghtya
				Past Participle
				dyghtyes

DYLLO (DYLLO): to send forth, discharge, publish, set free, set off (gun), unleash				
	Present	**Imperfect**	**Preterite**	**Pluperfect**
S 1	dyllaf	dyllyn	delles	dylsen
S 2	dyllyth	dyllys	dellessys	dylses
S 3	dyllo	dylly	dellos	dylosa
P 1	dyllyn	dyllyn	dellesen	dylsyn
P 2	dyllough	dylleugh	dellesough	dylseugh
P 3	dyllons	dyllens	dellesons	dylsens
0	dyllyr	dyllys	dellos	dylsys
	Present Subjunctive	**Imperfect Subjunctive**	**Imperative**	**Present Participle**
S 1	dyllyf	dellen		ow tyllo
S 2	dylly	delles	dyllo	
S 3	dyllosso	dyllossa	dyllens	**Past Participle**
P 1	dyllyn	dellen	dyllen	dyllys
P 2	dyllough	delleugh	dylleugh	
P 3	dellons	dellens	dyllens	
0	dyller	dyllys		

Examples: *dyllo gwyns* - to belch; *dyllo gos* - to let blood

DYNERGHY (DYNARGH): to welcome				
	Present	**Imperfect**	**Preterite**	**Pluperfect**
S3	dynergh	dynerghy	dynerghys	dynarghsa
	Present Subjunctive	**Imperfect Subjunctive**	**Imperative**	**Present Participle**
S3	dynargho	dynargha		ow tynerghy
				Past Participle
				dynerghys

DYSKY (DYSK): to learn, teach, educate, direct				
	Present	**Imperfect**	**Preterite**	**Pluperfect**
S 1	dyscaf	dyskyn	dyskys	dyssen
S 2	dyskyth	dyskys	dyssys	dysses
S 3	dysk	dysky	dyscas	dyssa
P 1	dyskyn	dyskyn	dyssyn	dyssen
P 2	dyscough	dyskeugh	dyssough	dysseugh
P 3	dyscons	dyskens	dyssons	dyssens
	Present Subjunctive	**Imperfect Subjunctive**	**Imperative**	**Present Participle**
S 1	dyskyf	dysken		ow tysky
S 2	dysky	dyskes	dysk	
S 3	dysco	dysca	dyskens	**Past Participle**
P 1	dyskyn	dysken	dyskyn	dyskys
P 2	dyscough	dyskeugh	dyskeugh	
P 3	dyscons	dyskens	dyskens	

Example: *dysky dhe - to teach; rag dysky dhedha* - to teach them
dysky gans - to learn; *may hyllyn genes dysky* - that I could learn from you

DYSPUTYA (DYSPUT): to argue				
	Present	**Imperfect**	**Preterite**	**Pluperfect**
S 3	dysput	dysputya	dysputyas	dysputsa
	Present Subjunctive	**Imperfect Subjunctive**	**Imperative**	**Present Participle**
S 3	dysputyo	dysputya		ow tysputya
				Past Participle
				dysputyes

N.B. Used with *orth*

DYSQUEDHES (DYSQUA): to show				
	Present	**Imperfect**	**Preterite**	**Pluperfect**
S 3	dysqua**	dysquedhy	dysquedhas	dysquethsa
	Present Subjunctive	**Imperfect Subjunctive**	**Imperative**	**Present Participle**
S 2			dysqua	ow tysquedhes
S 3	dysquetho	dysquetha		
				Past Participle
				dysquedhys

N.B. Used with *dhe* + 2nd state mutation. ***dysqueth before a vowel*

DYSTEMPRA (DYSTEMPER): to upset, vex				
	Present	**Imperfect**	**Preterite**	**Pluperfect**
S 3	dystemper	dystempra	dystempras	dystempersa
	Present Subjunctive	**Imperfect Subjunctive**	**Imperative**	**Present Participle**
S 3	dystempro	dystempra		ow tystempra
				Past Participle
				dystemprys

DYVYNYA (DYVYN): to chop, mince				
	Present	**Imperfect**	**Preterite**	**Pluperfect**
S 3	dyvyn	dyvynya	dyvynyas	dyvynsa
	Present Subjunctive	**Imperfect Subjunctive**	**Imperative**	**Present Participle**
S 3	dyvynyo	dyvynya		ow tyvynya
				Past Participle
				dyvynyes

DYWYSCA (DYWYSK): to undress				
	Present	**Imperfect**	**Preterite**	**Pluperfect**
S 3	dywysk	dywysca	dywyscas	dywyssa
	Present Subjunctive	**Imperfect Subjunctive**	**Imperative**	**Present Participle**
S 3	dyswysco	dywysca		ow tywysca
				Past Participle
				dywyskys

ENTRA (ENTER): to enter				
	Present	**Imperfect**	**Preterite**	**Pluperfect**
S 3	enter	entra	entras	entersa
	Present Subjunctive	**Imperfect Subjunctive**	**Imperative**	**Present Participle**
S 3	entro	entra		owth entra
				Past Participle
				entrys

N.B. Used with *dhe* + 2nd state mutation

ERBYSY (ERBYS): to save, economise				
	Present	**Imperfect**	**Preterite**	**Pluperfect**
S 3	erbys	erbysy	erbysys	erbyssa
	Present Subjunctive	**Imperfect Subjunctive**	**Imperative**	**Present Participle**
S 3	erbysso	erbysa		owth erbysy
				Past Participle
				erbysys

ERGHY (ARGH): to command				
	Present	**Imperfect**	**Preterite**	**Pluperfect**
S 1	arghaf			
S 3	ergh	erghy	erghys	arghsa
	Present Subjunctive	**Imperfect Subjunctive**	**Imperative**	**Present Participle**
S 2	erghy		argh	owth erghy
S 3	argho	argha		
				Past Participle
				erghys

N.B. Used with *dhe* + 2nd state mutation

ERVYRA (ERVYR): to decide, be convinced				
	Present	**Imperfect**	**Preterite**	**Pluperfect**
S 3	ervyr	ervyra	ervyras	ervyrsa
	Present Subjunctive	**Imperfect Subjunctive**	**Imperative**	**Present Participle**
S 3	ervyrro	ervyrra		owth ervyra
				Past Participle
				ervyrys

N.B. Used with *dhe* + 2nd state mutation
Example: *ervyrys of* - my mind is made up

ESEDHA (ESETH): to sit				
	Present	**Imperfect**	**Preterite**	**Pluperfect**
S 1	esedhaf, yth se' f	esedhen	esedhys	esethsen
S 2	esedhys	esedhes	esethsys	esethses
S 3	eseth, esa	esedha	esedhas	esethsa
P 1	esedhyn	esedhen	esethsyn	esethseugh
P 2	esedhough	esedheugh	esethsough	esethseugh
P 3	esedhons	esedhens	esethsons	esethsens
	Present Subjunctive	**Imperfect Subjunctive**	**Imperative**	**Present Participle**
S 1	esedhyf	esedhen		owth esedha
S 2	esedhy	esedhes	eseth, esa	
S 3	esetho	esetha	esedhens	**Past Participle**
P 1	esedhyn	esedhen	esedhyn	esedhys
P 2	esedhough	esedheugh	esedheugh	
P 3	esethons	esethens	esedhens	

EVA (YF): to drink				
	Present	**Imperfect**	**Preterite**	**Pluperfect**
S 3	yf	eva	evas	efsa
	Present Subjunctive	**Imperfect Subjunctive**	**Imperative**	**Present Participle**
S 2	yffy		yf	owth eva
S 3	effo	effa		
				Past Participle
				evys

EWNA (EWN): to make right, mend, amend, adjust, fit, arrange				
	Present	**Imperfect**	**Preterite**	**Pluperfect**
S 3	ewn	ewna	ewnas	ewnsa
	Present Subjunctive	**Imperfect Subjunctive**	**Imperative**	**Present Participle**
S 3	ewno	ewna		owth ewna
				Past Participle
				ewnys

FRONA (FRON): to curb, restrain				
	Present	**Imperfect**	**Preterite**	**Pluperfect**
S 3	fron	frona	fronas	fronsa
	Present Subjunctive	**Imperfect Subjunctive**	**Imperative**	**Present Participle**
S 3	fronno	fronna		ow frona
				Past Participle
				fronys

FRUDHA (FRUTH): to fray out, unravel				
	Present	**Imperfect**	**Preterite**	**Pluperfect**
S 3	fruth	frudha	frudhas	fruthsa
	Present Subjunctive	**Imperfect Subjunctive**	**Imperative**	**Present Participle**
S 3	frutho	frutha		ow frudha
				Past Participle
				frudhys

FUSTA (FUST): to thresh, give someone a thrashing				
	Present	**Imperfect**	**Preterite**	**Pluperfect**
S 3	fust	fusta	fustas	fustsa
	Present Subjunctive	**Imperfect Subjunctive**	**Imperative**	**Present Participle**
S 3	fusto	fusta		ow fusta
				Past Participle
				fustys

FYA (FY): to flee				
	Present	**Imperfect**	**Preterite**	**Pluperfect**
S 1	fyaf	fyen	fyys	fysen
S 2	fyyth	fyes	fysys	fyses
S 3	fy	fya	fyas	fysa
P 1	fyyn	fyen	fysyn	fysen
P 2	fyough	fyeugh	fysough	fyseugh
P 3	fyons	fyens	fysons	fysens
	Present Subjunctive	**Imperfect Subjunctive**	**Imperative**	**Present Participle**
S 1	fyyf	fyen		ow fya
S 2	fyy	fyes	fy	
S 3	fyo	fya	fyens	**Past Participle**
P 1	fyyn	fyen	fyyn	fyyes
P 2	fyough	fyeugh	fyeugh	
P 3	fyons	fyens	fyens	

N.B. Do not confuse with ***FYA : to despise, pour scorn on***

Verbs which follow the pattern of ***FYA: to flee***

With long 'y': a stem of two syllables, the vowel *"Y"*being part of the verb stem;

AFYA: ***to affirm***
ASWYA : ***to make a gap***
CRYA: ***to cry out (see p 26)***
DEFYA: ***to defy***
GOLYA: ***to wound***
GOWLYA: ***to commit perjury***
GWYA: ***to weave, knit, twine (see p 58)***
KERYA: ***to mend shoes***
LYA: ***to take an oath***
SYA: ***to buzz, hiss***
YNNYA: ***to urge, incite (see p 104)***

With short 'y': a stem of one syllable, the vowel *"Y"* not being part of the verb stem;

CHASTYA: ***to chastise***
CONTRADYA: ***to contradict***
COVYA: ***to breed, hatch chicks***
DUSTUNYA: ***to testify***
PONYA : ***to run (see p 81)***
PROVYA: ***to supply***
TARYA: ***to delay***

FYLLEL (FALL): to fail, lack, be found wanting				
	Present	**Imperfect**	**Preterite**	**Pluperfect**
S 1	fallaf			
S 3	fyll	fylly	fyllys	falsa
	Present Subjunctive	**Imperfect Subjunctive**	**Imperative**	**Present Participle**
S 2			fall	ow fyllel
S 3	fallo	falla		
				Past Participle
				fyllys

Example: *gwyn fyllys* - vinegar

FYSTYNA (FYSTYN) / FESTYNA (FESTYN): to hurry				
	Present	**Imperfect**	**Preterite**	**Pluperfect**
S 3	fystyn	fystyna	fystynas	fystynsa
	Present Subjunctive	**Imperfect Subjunctive**	**Imperative**	**Present Participle**
S 3	fystynno	fystynna		ow fystyna
				Past Participle
				fystynys

GARMA (GARM): to shout				
	Present	**Imperfect**	**Preterite**	**Pluperfect**
S 3	garm	garma	garmas	garmsa
	Present Subjunctive	**Imperfect Subjunctive**	**Imperative**	**Present Participle**
S 3	garmo	garma		ow carma
				Past Participle
				garmys

Example: *garma war* - to cry out

GASA (GAS): to leave, cease, abandon, permit				
	Present	**Imperfect**	**Preterite**	**Pluperfect**
S 1	gasaf	gasen	gesys	gassen
S 2	gesys	gases	gyssys, gysta	gasses
S 3	gas	gasa	gasas	gassa
P 1	gesyn	gasen	gessyn	gassen
P 2	gesough	gaseugh	gessough	gasseugh
P 3	gesons	gasens	gassons	gassens
	Present Subjunctive	**Imperfect Subjunctive**	**Imperative**	**Present Participle**
S 1	gyssyf	gassen		ow casa
S 2	gyssy	gasses	gas	
S 3	gasso	gassa	gasens	**Past Participle**
P 1	gyssyn	gassen	gesyn	gesys
P 2	gyssough	gasseugh	geseugh	
P 3	gassons	gassens	gasens	

N.B. used with *dhe* + 2nd state mutation
Example: *gas cres dhym* - leave me alone;
gasa covath - to lose recollection, forget;
gasa dhe strevya - to leave off arguing; *gasa cumyas* - to ask permission, leave

GAVA (GAF): to forgive, pardon				
	Present	**Imperfect**	**Preterite**	**Pluperfect**
S 3	gaf	gava	gavas	gafsa
	Present Subjunctive	**Imperfect Subjunctive**	**Imperative**	**Present Participle**
S 2			gaf	ow cava
S 3	gaffo	gava		
				Past Participle
				gyvys, gefys

N.B. Used with *dhe* + 2nd state mutation.

GELWEL (GALW): to call, invite. Also MERWEL (MARW)*: to die, expire, go out (of flame)				
	Present	***Imperfect***	***Preterite***	***Pluperfect***
S 1	galwaf	gelwyn	gelwys	gawlsen
S 2	gelwyth	gelwys	gelwsys**	gawlses
S 3	gelow	gelwy	gelwys	gawlsa
P 1	gelwyn	gelwyn	gelwsyn**	gawlsen
P 2	gelwough	gelweugh	gelwsough**	gawlseugh
P 3	gelwons	gelwens	gawlsons	gawlsens
	Present Subjunctive	**Imperfect Subjunctive**	**Imperative**	**Present Participle**
S 1	gylwyf	galwen		ow kelwel
S 2	gylwy	galwes	galw***	
S 3	galwo	galwa	gelwens	**Past Participle**
P 1	gylwyn	galwen	gelwyn	gylwys
P 2	gylwough	galweugh	gelweugh	
P 3	galwons	galwens	gelwens	

* 3rd person singular (S 3) Present Subjuntive of ***MERWEL*** – *marwo,* past participle - *marow/merow*

** Where the verbal ending starts with s the *w* is left silent

*** The w of *galw* is only sounded before a vowel - *galw y (gal'-wee)* - call them

GLANHE (GLANHA): to clean, clear				
	Present	**Imperfect**	**Preterite**	**Pluperfect**
S 1	glanhaf	glanhyn	glanhys	glanhasen
S 2	glanhyth	glanhys	glanhasys	glanhases
S 3	glanha	glanhy	glanhas	glanhasa
P 1	glanhyn	glanhyn	glanhasyn	glanhasen
P 2	glanhough	glanheugh	glanhasough	glanhaseugh
P 3	glanhons	glanhens	glanhasons	glanhasens
	Present Subjunctive	**Imperfect Subjunctive**	**Imperative**	**Present Participle**
S 1	glanhahyf	glanhahen		ow clanhe
S 2	glanhahy	glanhahes	glanha	
S 3	glanhaho	glanhaha	glanhens	**Past Participle**
P 1	glanhahyn	glanhahen	glanhen	glanhes
P 2	glanhahough	glanhaheugh	glanheugh	
P 3	glanhahons	glanhahens	glanhens	

N.B. For other verbs like ***GLANHE*** with adjective + *-he* suffix see page 107

GLENA (GLEN): to cling, stick, adhere to				
	Present	**Imperfect**	**Preterite**	**Pluperfect**
S 3	glen	glena	glennas	glensa
	Present Subjunctive	**Imperfect Subjunctive**	**Imperative**	**Present Participle**
S 3	glenno	glena		ow clena
				Past Participle
				glenys

N.B. Used with *orth*

GOLGHY (GOLGH): to wash				
	Present	**Imperfect**	**Preterite**	**Pluperfect**
S 3	golgh	golghy	golghas	golghsa
	Present Subjunctive	**Imperfect Subjunctive**	**Imperative**	**Present Participle**
S 3	golgho	golgha		ow golghy
				Past Participle
				golgh

N.B. See also reflexive verb
OMWOLGHY (OMWOLGH): to wash oneself page 78

GOLYA (GOL): to sail				
	Present	**Imperfect**	**Preterite**	**Pluperfect**
S 3	gol	golya	golyas	golsa
	Present Subjunctive	**Imperfect Subjunctive**	**Imperative**	**Present Participle**
S 3	golyo	golya		ow colya
				Past Participle

N.B. Do not confuse with ***GOLYA (GOL): to feast***
or ***GOLYA (GOLY): to wound, hurt***

GONYS (GONYS): to work, cultivate				
	Present	**Imperfect**	**Preterite**	**Pluperfect**
S 1	gonedhaf			gonethsen
S 3	gonys	gonysy	gonedhas	gonethsa
	Present Subjunctive	**Imperfect Subjunctive**	**Imperative**	**Present Participle**
S 2			gonys	
S 3	gonetho	gonetha		ow conys
				Past Participle
				gonedhys

GORLENWEL (GORLANW): to overfill				
	Present	**Imperfect**	**Preterite**	**Pluperfect**
S 3	gorlen	gorleny	gorlenys	gorlensa
	Present Subjunctive	**Imperfect Subjunctive**	**Imperative**	**Present Participle**
S 3	gorlanwo	gorlanwa		ow corlenwel
				Past Participle
				gorlenwys

N.B. Used with *gans* or *a* + 2nd state mutation

GORLYWA (GORLYW): to overcolour, exaggerate				
	Present	**Imperfect**	**Preterite**	**Pluperfect**
S 3	gorlyw	gorlywa	gorlewas	gorlewsa
	Present Subjunctive	**Imperfect Subjunctive**	**Imperative**	**Present Participle**
S 3	gorlewo	gorlewa		ow corlywa
				Past Participle
				gorlewys

GORRA (GOR): to place, put, set				
	Present	**Imperfect**	**Preterite**	**Pluperfect**
S 3	gor	gorra	gorras	gorsa
	Present Subjunctive	**Imperfect Subjunctive**	**Imperative**	**Present Participle**
S 3	gorro	gorra		ow corra
				Past Participle
				gorrys

Example: *gorra dhe dhyscans* - to educate;
gorra wyth a/dhe - to take care of/to

GORTHEBY (GORTHYB): to reply, answer, retaliate				
	Present	**Imperfect**	**Preterite**	**Pluperfect**
S 1	gorthebaf	gorthebyn	gorthebys	gorthepsen
S 2	gorthebys	gorthebys	gorthepsys	gorthepses
S 3	gorthyp	gortheby	gorthebys	gorthepsa
P 1	gorthebyn	gorthebyn	gorthepsyn	gorthepsen
P 2	gorthebough	gorthebeugh	gorthepsough	gorthepseugh
P 3	gorthebons	gorthebens	gorthepsons	gorthepsens
	Present Subjunctive	**Imperfect Subjunctive**	**Imperative**	**Present Participle**
S 1	gorthebyf	gortheben		ow cortheby
S 2	gortheby	gorthebes	gorthyb	
S 3	gortheppo	gortheppa	gorthebens	**Past Participle**
P 1	gorthebon	gortheben	gorthebyn	gorthebys
P 2	gorthebough	gorthebeugh	gorthebeugh	
P 3	gortheppons	gortheppens	gorthebens	

N.B. Used with or without *orth*

GORTOS (GORTA): to wait, stop, delay				
	Present	**Imperfect**	**Preterite**	**Pluperfect**
S 3	gorta	gortos	gortas	gortsa
	Present Subjunctive	**Imperfect Subjunctive**	**Imperative**	**Present Participle**
S 2			gorta	ow cortos
S 3	gorto	gorta		
P 2			gorteugh	
				Past Participle

GOSLOWES (GOSLOW): to hear, listen to, pay attention				
	Present	**Imperfect**	**Preterite**	**Pluperfect**
S 3	goslow	goslowy	goslowas	goslowsa
	Present Subjunctive	**Imperfect Subjunctive**	**Imperative**	**Present Participle**
S 2			goslow	ow coslowes
S 3	goslowo	goslowa	goslewys	
P 2			gosloweugh	
				Past Participle

N.B. Used with *orth,* sometimes *dhe* + 2nd state mutation

GOTHVOS (GOTH): to know (for a fact), know how				
	Present	**Imperfect**	**Preterite***	**Pluperfect**
S 1	gon	godhyen	gothfef	gothfyen
S 2	godhes	godhyes	gothfes	gothfyes
S 3	gor	godhya	gothfe	gothfya
P 1	godhon	godhyen	gothfen	gothfyen
P 2	godhough	godhyeugh	gothfeugh	gothfyeugh
P 3	godhons	godhyens	gothfons	gothfyens
0	godhyr			

	Present Subjunctive	**Imperfect Subjunctive**	**Future**	**Imperative**	**Present Participle**
S 1	gothfyf	gothfen	gothvydhaf		ow cothvos
S 2	gothfy	gothfes	gothvydhyth	gothvyth	
S 3	gothfo	gothfa	gothvyth	gothvedhens	**Past Participle**
P 1	gothfen	gothfen	gothvydhyn	gothvedhen	gothvedhys
P 2	gothfeugh	gothfeugh	gothvydhough	gothvedheugh	
P 3	gothfons	gothfens	gothvydhons	gothvedhens	
0	godher				

*Preterite is unattested, use ***GUL*** + infinitive e.g *my a wruk gothvos* - I realised
N.B. Used with *yn, dhe* + 2nd state mutation, *a* + 2nd state mutation.
The imperatives *gothvyth* and *gothvedheugh* are used to mean beware!
Example: *gothvos gras* - to be grateful

GOVYN (GOVYN): to ask				
	Present	**Imperfect**	**Preterite**	**Pluperfect**
S 2	goventa (with suffixed pronoun)			
S 3	govyn	govyna	govynnas, govynnys	govensa
	Present Subjunctive	**Imperfect Subjunctive**	**Imperative**	**Present Participle**
S 3	govenno	govenna		ow covyn
				Past Participle
				govynnys

N.B. Used with *orth*
Example: *ef a wovynnas orth y wrek* - he asked (of) his wife
Can be made reflexive with prefix *om* – ***OMWOVYN: to wonder, ask oneself***

GRASSA (GRAS): to thank				
	Present	**Imperfect**	**Preterite**	**Pluperfect**
S 3	gras	grassa	grassas	grassa
	Present Subjunctive	**Imperfect Subjunctive**	**Imperative**	**Present Participle**
S 2			grassa	ow crassa
S 3	grasso	grassa		
				Past Participle
				grassys

N.B. Used with *dhe* + 2nd state mutation

GWARY (GWARY): to play				
	Present	**Imperfect**	**Preterite**	**Pluperfect**
S 3	gwary	gwary	gwaryas	gwarysa
	Present Subjunctive	**Imperfect Subjunctive**	**Imperative**	**Present Participle**
S 2			gwary	
S 3	gwaryo	gwarya		ow quary
				Past Participle
				gwaryys, gwaryes

GWAYA (GWAY): to move, stir				
	Present	**Imperfect**	**Preterite**	**Pluperfect**
S 3	gway	gwaya	gwayas	gwaysa
	Present Subjunctive	**Imperfect Subjunctive**	**Imperative**	**Present Participle**
S 3	gwayo	gwaya		ow quaya
				Past Participle
				gwayys

GWAYTYA (GWAYT): to wait, expect, hope				
	Present	**Imperfect**	**Preterite**	**Pluperfect**
S 3	gwayt	gwaytya	gwaytyas	gwaytsa
	Present Subjunctive	**Imperfect Subjunctive**	**Imperative**	**Present Participle**
S 3	gwaytyo	gwaytya		ow quaytya
				Past Participle
				gwaytyes

N.B. Used with *rak*

GWELES (GWEL): to see				
	Present	**Imperfect**	**Preterite**	**Pluperfect**
S 1	gwelaf	gwelyn	gwelys	gwelsen
S 2	gwelyth/gwelta	gwelys	gwelsys	gwelses
S 3	gwel	gwely	gwelas	gwelsa
P 1	gwelyn	gwelyn	gwelsyn	gwelsen
P 2	gwelough	gweleugh	gwelsough	gwelseugh
P 3	gwelons	gwelens	gwelsons	gwelsens
	Present Subjunctive	**Imperfect Subjunctive**	**Imperative**	**Present Participle**
S 1	gwyllyf	gwellen		ow queles
S 2	gwylly	gwelles	gwel	
S 3	gwello	gwella	gwelens	**Past Participle**
P 1	gwyllyn	gwellen	gwelyn	gwelys
P 2	gwellough	gwelleugh	gweleugh	
P 3	gwellons	gwellens	gwelens	

N.B. In Future tense only 3rd person sing (S 3) is found:
gwelvyth (my a welvyth) . Used with *rak*

GWERES (GWERES): to help				
	Present	**Imperfect**	**Preterite**	**Pluperfect**
S 3	gweres	gweresy	gweresas	gweressa
	Present Subjunctive	**Imperfect Subjunctive**	**Imperative**	**Present Participle**
S 3	gweresso	gweressa		ow queres
				Past Participle
				gweresys

N.B. Used with *orth*
Example: *ef a wra gweres orth y wul* - he is going to help you do it
N.B. Used with *dhe*
Example: *gweres dhym* - help me; *gweres ow cul* - to help to make

GWERTHA (GWERTH): to sell				
	Present	**Imperfect**	**Preterite**	**Pluperfect**
S 3	gwerth	gwertha	gwerthas	gwerthsa
	Present Subjunctive	**Imperfect Subjunctive**	**Imperative**	**Present Participle**
S 3	gwertho	gwertha		ow quertha
				Past Participle
				gwerthys

N.B. Used with *a* + 2nd state mutation or *orth*

GWESKEL (GWASK)/GWYSKEL: to strike				
	Present	**Imperfect**	**Preterite**	**Pluperfect**
S 1	gwascaf		gwyskys	
S 2			gwyssys	
S 3	gwesk, gwysk	gwesky	gwe(y)skys	gwasksa
	Present Subjunctive	**Imperfect Subjunctive**	**Imperative**	**Present Participle**
S 2			gwask	ow queskel
S 3	gwasco	gwasca		
				Past Participle
				gweskys, gwyskys

GWEVYA (GWEV): to flee, wander, become a vagrant				
	Present	**Imperfect**	**Preterite**	**Pluperfect**
S 3	gwev	gwevya	gwevyas	gwefsa
	Present Subjunctive	**Imperfect Subjunctive**	**Imperative**	**Present Participle**
S 3	gweffo	gweffa		ow quevya
				Past Participle
				gwevys

GWYA (GWY): to weave, knit, twine				
	Present	**Imperfect**	**Preterite**	**Pluperfect**
S 3	gwy	gwya	gwyas	gwysa
	Present Subjunctive	**Imperfect Subjunctive**	**Imperative**	**Present Participle**
S 3	gwysso	gwyssa		ow quya
				Past Participle
				gwyes

Example: *omwya adro dhe* - to twine around (climbing plant)

GWYSCA (GWYSK): to wear				
	Present	**Imperfect**	**Preterite**	**Pluperfect**
S 3	gwysk	gwysca	gwyscas	gwyssa
	Present Subjunctive	**Imperfect Subjunctive**	**Imperative**	**Present Participle**
S 3	gwysco	gwysca		ow quysca
				Past Participle
				gwyskys

GWYSTLA (GWYSTEL): to pledge				
	Present	**Imperfect**	**Preterite**	**Pluperfect**
S 1	gwystlaf	gwystlen	gwystlys	gwystelsen
S 2	gwystlyth	gwystles	gwystelsys	gwystelses
S 3	gwystel	gwystla	gwystlas	gwystelsa
P 1	gwystlyn	gwystlen	gwystelsyn	gwystelsen
P 2	gwystlough	gwystleugh	gwystelsough	gwystelseugh
P 3	gwystlons	gwystlens	gwystelsons	gwystelsens
0	gwystlyr	gwystlys	gwystlas	gwystelsys
	Present Subjunctive	**Imperfect Subjunctive**	**Imperative**	**Present Participle**
S 1	gwystlyf	gwystlen		ow quystla
S 2	gwystly	gwystles	gwystel	
S 3	gwystlo	gwystla	gwystlens	**Past Participle**
P 1	gwystlyn	gwystlen	gwystlyn	gwystlys
P 2	gwystlough	gwystleugh	gwystleugh	
P 3	gwystlons	gwystlens	gwystlens	
0	gwystler	gwystlys	-	

GWYTHA (GWYTH): to keep, guard, protect				
	Present	**Imperfect**	**Preterite**	**Pluperfect**
S 3	gwyth	gwytha	gwythas	gwythsa
	Present Subjunctive	**Imperfect Subjunctive**	**Imperative**	**Present Participle**
S 3	gwytho	gwytha		ow quytha
				Past Participle
				gwythys

N.B. Used with *orth, dhe, rak*

Example: *gwytha dhe* - to keep to; *gwytha war* - watch over
gwytha orth - guard against, protect; *gwytha erbyn* - keep until

Do not confuse with ***GWYTHA: to work, set working, exploit***

HANAJA (HANAJ): to sigh				
	Present	**Imperfect**	**Preterite**	**Pluperfect**
S 3	hanaj	hanaja	hanajas	hanachsa
	Present Subjunctive	**Imperfect Subjunctive**	**Imperative**	**Present Participle**
S 3	hanacho	hanacha		ow hanaja
				Past Participle
				hanajys

HAVY (HAF): to take a (summer) holiday				
	Present	**Imperfect**	**Preterite**	**Pluperfect**
S 3	haf	havy	havys	hafsa
	Present Subjunctive	**Imperfect Subjunctive**	**Imperative**	**Present Participle**
S 3	haffo	haffa		ow havy
				Past Participle
				havyes

HEDHES (HETH): to reach, extend, fetch, hand to another				
	Present	**Imperfect**	**Preterite**	**Pluperfect**
S 3	heth	hedha	hedhas	hethsa
	Present Subjunctive	**Imperfect Subjunctive**	**Imperative**	**Present Participle**
S 2			heth	ow hedhes
S 3	hetho	hetha		
				Past Participle
				hedhys

HEDHY (HETH): to stop, cease, halt				
	Present	**Imperfect**	**Preterite**	**Pluperfect**
S 3	heth	hedhy	hedhys	hethsa
	Present Subjunctive	**Imperfect Subjunctive**	**Imperative**	**Present Participle**
S 3	hetho	hethe		ow hedhy
P 2			hedheugh	
				Past Participle
				hedhys

Example: *kens es hedhy* - before resting, without stopping

HEMBRONK (HEMBRONK): to lead, conduct, bring				
	Present	**Imperfect**	**Preterite**	**Pluperfect**
S 3	hembronk	hembrynky	hembroncas	hembronksa
	Present Subjunctive	**Imperfect Subjunctive**	**Imperative**	**Present Participle**
S 3	hembronco	hembronca		ow hembronk
				Past Participle
				hembrynkys

HENWEL (HANW): to name				
	Present	***Imperfect***	***Preterite***	***Pluperfect***
S 1	hanwaf	henwyn	henwys	hawnsen
S 2	henwyth	henwys	henwsys**	hawnses
S 3	henow	henwy	henwys	hawnsa
P 1	henwyn	henwyn	henwsyn**	hawnsen
P 2	henwough	henweugh	henwsough**	hawnseugh
P 3	henwons	henwens	hanwsons	hawnsens
	Present Subjunctive	**Imperfect Subjunctive**	**Imperative**	**Present Participle**
S 1	hynwyf	hanwen		ow henwel
S 2	hynwy	hanwes	hanw***	
S 3	hanwo	hanwa	henwens	**Past Participle**
P 1	hynwyn	hanwen	henwyn	hynwys
P 2	hynwough	hanweugh	henweugh	
P 3	hanwons	hanwens	henwens	

N.B. Used with *orth,* Past Participle *hynwys* also means "set apart" or "sacred"
** Where the verb ending starts with *s* the *w* is left silent
*** The *w* of *henw* is only sounded before vowel - *henw y (hen'-wee)* - name them

HERDHYA (HORTH): to push, ram, thrust				
	Present	**Imperfect**	**Preterite**	**Pluperfect**
S 1	hordhyaf			
S 3	herth	herdhya	hordhas	horthsa
	Present Subjunctive	**Imperfect Subjunctive**	**Imperative**	**Present Participle**
S 2			horth	ow herdhya
S 3	herdhyo	herdhya		
				Past Participle
				herdhys

N.B. Used with *dhe*
Example: *herdhya dhe ves* - to launch (a boat)
N.B. Used with *orth*
Example: *herdhya orth* – to ram against

HUDA (HUS): to charm, enchant				
	Present	**Imperfect**	**Preterite**	**Pluperfect**
S 3	hus	huda	hudas	hutsa
	Present Subjunctive	**Imperfect Subjunctive**	**Imperative**	**Present Participle**
S 3	husso	hussa		ow huda
				Past Participle
				hudys

HURLYA (HURL): to hurl (sport)				
	Present	**Imperfect**	**Preterite**	**Pluperfect**
S 3	hurl	hurlya	hurlyas	hurlsa
	Present Subjunctive	**Imperfect Subjunctive**	**Imperative**	**Present Participle**
S 3	hurlyo	hurlya		ow hurlya
				Past Participle
				hurlyes

JUNNYA (JOYN): to join, put together with others				
	Present	**Imperfect**	**Preterite**	**Pluperfect**
S 3	joyn	junnya	junnyas	junsa
	Present Subjunctive	**Imperfect Subjunctive**	**Imperative**	**Present Participle**
S 3	junnyo	junnya		ow junnya
				Past Participle
				junnyes

KELES (KEL): to hide, conceal, keep secret				
	Present	**Imperfect**	**Preterite**	**Pluperfect**
S 3	kel	kely	kelas	kelsa
	Present Subjunctive	**Imperfect Subjunctive**	**Imperative**	**Present Participle**
S 2			kel	ow keles
S 3	kello	kella		
				Past Participle
				kelys

KELLY (COLL): to lose				
	Present	**Imperfect**	**Preterite**	**Pluperfect**
S.3	kell	kelly	collas	collsa
	Present Subjunctive	**Imperfect Subjunctive**	**Imperative**	**Present Participle**
S 2			coll	ow kelly
S 3	collo	colla		
				Past Participle
				kellys, kyllys

N.B. Used with *orth*

KELMY (COLM): to tie, knot, oblige				
	Present	**Imperfect**	**Preterite**	**Pluperfect**
S 3	kelm	kelmy	colmas	colmsa
	Present Subjunctive	**Imperfect Subjunctive**	**Imperative**	**Present Participle**
S 2			colm	ow kelmy
S 3	colmo	colma		
				Past Participle
				kelmys

N.B. Used with *dhe*+ 2nd state mutation, *orth*
Example: *kelmy dhe* - bound for, on the way to

KEMERES (KEMER): to take, receive, accept				
	Present	**Imperfect**	**Preterite**	**Pluperfect**
S 1	kemeraf	kemeryn	kemerys	kemersen
S 2	kemerys	kemerys	kemersys	kemerses
S 3	kemer	kemery	kemeras	kemersa
P 1	kemeryn	kemeryn	kemersyn	kemersen
P 2	kemerough	kemereugh	kemersough	kemerseugh
P 3	kemerons	kemerens	kemersons	kemersens
	Present Subjunctive	**Imperfect Subjunctive**	**Imperative**	**Present Participle**
S 1	kemyrryf	kemerren		ow kemeres
S 2	kemyrry	kemerres	kemer	
S 3	kemerro	kemerra	kemerens	**Past Participle**
P 1	kemerren	kemerren	kemeryn	kemerys
P 2	kemerrough	kemerreugh	kemereugh	
P 3	kemerrons	kemerrens	kemerens	

Example: *kemeres gallos* - to assume power;
kemeres ynban - to rise and leave the table

KENTRA (KENTER): to nail, spike				
	Present	**Imperfect**	**Preterite**	**Pluperfect**
S 3	kenter	kentra	kentras	kentersa
	Present Subjunctive	**Imperfect Subjunctive**	**Imperative**	**Present Participle**
S 2			kenter	ow kentra
S 3	kenterro	kenterra		
				Past Participle
				kentrys

N.B. Use *kentr'* before vowels. Used with *orth*
Example: *my a's kenter orth an lur* - I will nail it to the floor

KERDHES (KERTH): to walk				
	Present	**Imperfect**	**Preterite**	**Pluperfect**
S 3	kerth	kerdhy	kerdhas	kerthsa
	Present Subjunctive	**Imperfect Subjunctive**	**Imperative**	**Present Participle**
S 3	kertho	kertha		ow kerdhes
				Past Participle
				kerdhys

Example: *ke dhe gerdhes* - be off, get out

KEREDHY (KERETH): to chastise, rebuke, correct				
	Present	**Imperfect**	**Preterite**	**Pluperfect**
S 3	kereth	keredhy	keredhas	kerthsa
	Present Subjunctive	**Imperfect Subjunctive**	**Imperative**	**Present Participle**
S 3	keretho	keretha		ow keredhy
				Past Participle
				keredhys

KESKY (COSK): to advise, exhort, admonish				
	Present	**Imperfect**	**Preterite**	**Pluperfect**
S 3	kesk	kesky	coscas	cossa
	Present Subjunctive	**Imperfect Subjunctive**	**Imperative**	**Present Participle**
S 2			kosk, cosk	ow kesky
S 3	cosco	cosca		
				Past Participle
				keskys

KEWSEL (KEWS/COWS): to speak, talk, converse* *Also KESKEWSEL: to talk together*				
	Present	**Imperfect**	**Preterite**	**Pluperfect**
S 1	cowsaf	kewsyn	kewsys	cowssen
S 2	kewsyth	kewsys	kewssys	cowsses
S 3	kews	kewsy	kewsys / cowsas	cowssa
P 1	kewsyn	kewsyn	kewssyn	cowssen
P 2	kewsough	kewseugh	kewssough	cowsseugh
P 3	kewsons	kewsens	cowssons	cowssens
	Present Subjunctive	**Imperfect Subjunctive**	**Imperative**	**Present Participle**
S 1	kewsyf	cowsen		ow kewsel
S 2	kewsy	cowses	cows	
S 3	cowso	cowsa	kewsens /cowsens	**Past Participle**
P 1	kewsyn	cowsen	kewsyn/cowsyn	kewsys
P 2	kewsough	cowseugh	kewseugh/ cowseugh	
P 3	cowsons	cowsens	kewsens/cowsens	

*Use *kews* or *cows* as a stem - (*cows* is later Cornish)
N.B. *dhe* + 2nd state mutation or *gans, orth*
Example: *kewsel orth* - to speak to, talk to;
kewsel gans - to speak in favour of, defend

KYJYA (KYJ): to join, stick fast, unite, **modern usage - *to engage in sexual intercourse***				
	Present	**Imperfect**	**Preterite**	**Pluperfect**
S 3	kyj	kyjya	kyjyas	kychsa
	Present Subjunctive	**Imperfect Subjunctive**	**Imperative**	**Present Participle**
S 3	kychyo	kychya		ow kyjya
				Past Participle
				kyjyes

N.B. Used with *orth*

LADRA (LADER): to steal, rob, thieve				
	Present	**Imperfect**	**Preterite**	**Pluperfect**
S 1	ladraf	ladren	ledrys	latsen
S 2	ledryth	ladres	letsys	latses
S 3	lader	ladra	ladras	latsa
P 1	ledryn	ladren	letsyn	latsen
P 2	ledrough	ladreugh	letsough	latseugh
P 3	ladrons	ladrens	latsons	latsens
	Present Subjunctive	**Imperfect Subjunctive**	**Imperative**	**Present Participle**
S 1	lyttryf	lattren		ow ladra
S 2	lyttry	lattres	lader	
S 3	lattro	lattra	ladrens	**Past Participle**
P 1	lyttryn	lattren	ledryn	ledrys
P 2	lyttrough	lattreugh	ledreugh	
P 3	lattrons	lattrens	ladrens	

N.B. No contraction in Preterite or Pluperfect in conjugations of
WHYSTRA (WHYSTER) ***GWANDRA (GWANDER)*** ***GWYSTLA (GWYSTEL)***
e.g . *whystersys* *gwandersough* *gwystelsons*
Also 3rd person singular (S 3) Present Future
WHYSTRA (whisper) - *whyster* ***GWANDRA*** (wander) - *gwander*
GUSTLA (riot) - *gustel* ***GWYSTLA*** (pledge, pawn)- *gwystel*
TERLENTRY (shine) - *terlenter* ***SUGNA*** (suck) - *sugen*

LAMMA (LAM): to leap, hop, stride, jump, bound				
	Present	**Imperfect**	**Preterite**	**Pluperfect**
S 3	lam	lamma	lammas	lamsa
	Present Subjunctive	**Imperfect Subjunctive**	**Imperative**	**Present Participle**
S 2			lam	
S 3	lammo	lamma		ow lamma
				Past Participle
				lemmys

N.B. Used with *dres*

LEMMEL (LAM): to leap, hop, jump, stride, bound				
	Present	**Imperfect**	**Preterite**	**Pluperfect**
S 3	lem	lemma	lemmys	lemsa
	Present Subjunctive	**Imperfect Subjunctive**	**Imperative**	**Present Participle**
S 2			lam	ow lemmel
S 3	lemmo	lemma		
				Past Participle
				lemmys

LENKY (LONK): to swallow *Also COLLENKY (COLLONK): to swallow completely*				
	Present	**Imperfect**	**Preterite**	**Pluperfect**
S 3	lenk	lenky	loncas	lonksa
	Present Subjunctive	**Imperfect Subjunctive**	**Imperative**	**Present Participle**
S 2			lonk	
S 3	lonco	lonca		ow lenky
				Past Participle
				lenkys

LENWEL (LANW): to fill, replenish ***Also COLLENWEL (COLLANW): to complete, fulfil, satisfy, accomplish*** ***Also MORLENWEL (MORLANW): to rise, flow (tide)***				
	Present	**Imperfect**	**Preterite**	**Pluperfect**
S 1	lanwaf	lenwyn	lenwys	lawnsen
S 2	lenwyth	lenwys	lenwsys**	lawnses
S 3	lenow	lenwy	lenwys	lawnsa
P 1	lenwyn	lenwyn	lenwsyn**	lawnsen
P 2	lenwough	lenweugh	lensough	lawnseugh
P 3	lenwons	lenwens	lawnsons	lawnsens
0	lenwyr	lensys	lenwys	lawnsys
	Present Subjunctive	**Imperfect Subjunctive**	**Imperative**	**Present Participle**
S 1	lenwyf	lanwen		ow lenwel
S 2	lenwy	lanwes	lanow	
S 3	lanwo	lanwa	lenwens	
P 1	lenwyn	lanwen	lenwyn	
P 2	lenwough	lanweugh	lenweugh	**Past Participle**
P 3	lanwons	lanwens	lenwens	lenwys
0	lanwer	lenwys		

** where the verb ending begins with *s* the *w* is left silent

N.B. Usually used with *a* + 2nd state mutation or *gans*

Example: *lenwel a* - to fill with

LESTA (LEST): to prevent, hinder				
	Present	**Imperfect**	**Preterite**	**Pluperfect**
S 1	lestaf	lesten	lestys	lessen
S 2	lestyth	lestes	lessys	lesses
S 3	lest	lesta	lestas	lessa
P 1	lestyn	lesten	lessyn	lessen
P 2	lestough	lesteugh	lessough	lesseugh
P 3	lestons	lestens	lessons	lessens
	Present Subjunctive	**Imperfect Subjunctive**	**Imperative**	**Present Participle**
S 1	lestyf	lesten		ow lesta
S 2	lesty	lestes	lest	
S 3	lesto	lesta	lestens	**Past Participle**
P 1	lestyn	lesten	lestyn	lestys
P 2	lestough	lesteugh	lesteugh	
P 3	lestons	lestens	lestens	

N.B. Used with *rak*

LEVEREL (LAVAR): to say, tell, relate				
	Present	**Imperfect**	**Preterite**	**Pluperfect**
S 1	lavaraf	leveryn	leverys	lavarsen
S 2	leveryth	leverys	leversys	lavarses
S 3	lever	levery	leverys	lavarsa
P 1	leveryn	leveryn	leversyn	lavarsen
P 2	leverough	levereugh	leversough	lavarseugh
P 3	leverons	leverens	lavarsons	lavarsens
	Present Subjunctive	**Imperfect Subjunctive**	**Imperative**	**Present Participle**
S 1	leverryf	lavarren		ow leverel
S 2	leverry	lavarres	lavar	
S 3	lavarro	lavarra	leverens	**Past Participle**
P 1	leverryn	lavarren	leveryn	leverys
P 2	leverrough	lavarreugh	levereugh	
P 3	lavarrons	lavarrens	leverens	

N.B. Used with *dhe* or *a* + 2nd state mutation
Example: *leverel dhe* - to tell to/about

LEWYAS (LEW): to drive, steer, guide, direct				
	Present	**Imperfect**	**Preterite**	**Pluperfect**
S 3	lew	lewy	lewas	lewsa
	Present Subjunctive	**Imperfect Subjunctive**	**Imperative**	**Present Participle**
S 3	lewo	lewa		ow lewyas
				Past Participle
				lewys

MAYLYA (MAYL): to wrap in a cloth, swathe, bandage				
	Present	**Imperfect**	**Preterite**	**Pluperfect**
S 3	mayl	maylya	maylyas	maylsa
	Present Subjunctive	**Imperfect Subjunctive**	**Imperative**	**Present Participle**
S 3	maylyo	maylya		ow maylya
				Past Participle
				maylyes

MENEGES (MENEK): to point out, mention, report				
	Present	**Imperfect**	**Preterite**	**Pluperfect**
S 3	menek	menegy	menegas	meneksa
	Present Subjunctive	**Imperfect Subjunctive**	**Imperative**	**Present Participle**
S 3	menecco	menecca		ow meneges
				Past Participle
				menegys

MENTENA (MENTEN): to stand by, uphold, maintain				
	Present	**Imperfect**	**Preterite**	**Pluperfect**
S 3	menten	mentena	mentenas	mentensa
	Present Subjunctive	**Imperfect Subjunctive**	**Imperative**	**Present Participle**
S 3	mentenno	mentenna		ow mentena
				Past Participle
				mentenys

MORA (MOR): to put to sea, launch, sail				
	Present	**Imperfect**	**Preterite**	**Pluperfect**
S 3	mor	mora	moras	morsa
	Present Subjunctive	**Imperfect Subjunctive**	**Imperative**	**Present Participle**
S 3	morro	morra		ow mora
				Past Participle
				morys

N.B. Do not confuse with ***MORA: to go blackberrying***

MUVYA (MUF): to move, stir, incite, propose ***Also AMUVYA (AMUF): to perturb, agitate, startle, cause emotion in*** ***Also REMUVYA (REMUF): to remove, change place***				
	Present	**Imperfect**	**Preterite**	**Pluperfect**
S 3	muf	muvya	muvyas	mufsa
	Present Subjunctive	**Imperfect Subjunctive**	**Imperative**	**Present Participle**
S 3	mufyo	mufya		ow muvya
				Past Participle
				muvyes

MYJY (MYJ): to reap				
	Present	**Imperfect**	**Preterite**	**Pluperfect**
S 3	myj	myjy	myjas	mychsa
	Present Subjunctive	**Imperfect Subjunctive**	**Imperative**	**Present Participle**
S 3	mycho	mycha		ow myjy
				Past Participle
				myjys

MYRAS (MYR): to look, behold, consider				
	Present	**Imperfect**	**Preterite**	**Pluperfect**
S 3	myr	myras	myrys	myrsa
	Present Subjunctive	**Imperfect Subjunctive**	**Imperative**	**Present Participle**
S 2			myr	ow myras
S 3	myrro	myrra		
				Past Participle
				myrys

N.B. Used with *dhe* + 2nd state mutation, *orth*

NAGHA (NAGH): to deny, refuse, recant				
	Present	**Imperfect**	**Preterite**	**Pluperfect**
S 3	nagh	nagha	naghas	naghsa
P 1	neghyn			
	Present Subjunctive	**Imperfect Subjunctive**	**Imperative**	**Present Participle**
S 3	nagho	nagha		ow nagha
				Past Participle
				neghys

Example: *nagh y!* - deny them!

NESHE (NESHA): to come or bring nearer				
	Present	**Imperfect**	**Preterite**	**Pluperfect**
S 1	neshaf	neshyn	neshys	neshasen
S 2	neshyth	neshys	neshasys	neshases
S 3	nesha	neshy	neshas	neshasa
P 1	neshyn	neshyn	neshasyn	neshasen
P 2	neshough	nesheugh	neshasough	neshaseugh
P 3	neshons	neshens	neshasons	neshasens
	Present Subjunctive	**Imperfect Subjunctive**	**Imperative**	**Present Participle**
S 1	neshahyf	neshahen		ow neshe
S 2	neshahy	neshahes	nesha	
S 3	neshaho	neshaha	neshes, neshens	**Past Participle**
P 1	neshahyn	neshahen	neshen	neshe, neshys
P 2	neshahough	neshaheugh	nesheugh	
P 3	neshahons	neshahens	neshens	

N.B. For other verbs like ***NESHE*** with adjective + *-he* suffix see page 107

NESSA (NES): to draw near, approach				
	Present	**Imperfect**	**Preterite**	**Pluperfect**
S 3	nes	nessa	nessas	nessa
	Present Subjunctive	**Imperfect Subjunctive**	**Imperative**	**Present Participle**
S 2			nes	ow nessa
S 3	nesso	nessa		
				Past Participle

NOTHHE (NOTHHA): to bare				
	Present	**Imperfect**	**Preterite**	**Pluperfect**
S 3	nothha	nothhy	nothhas	nothhasa
	Present Subjunctive	**Imperfect Subjunctive**	**Imperative**	**Present Participle**
S 3	nothhaho	nothhaha		ow nothhe
				Past Participle
				nothhes

NYJA (NYJ) / NYJYA (NYJY): to swim, float, fly				
	Present	**Imperfect**	**Preterite**	**Pluperfect**
S 3	nyj	nyja	nyjyas	nychsa
	Present Subjunctive	**Imperfect Subjunctive**	**Imperative**	**Present Participle**
S 3	nycho	nycha		ow nyja
P 2			nyjeugh	
				Past Participle
				nyjys/ nyjyes (afloat, floating)

OBAYA (OBAY): to yield, surrender, obey, submit				
	Present	**Imperfect**	**Preterite**	**Pluperfect**
S 3	obay	obaya	obayas	obaysa
	Present Subjunctive	**Imperfect Subjunctive**	**Imperative**	**Present Participle**
S 3	obayo	obaya		owth obaya
				Past Participle
				obayys

N.B. Used with *dhe* + 2nd state mutation

OLA (OL): to cry, weep, lament, repent				
	Present	**Imperfect**	**Preterite**	**Pluperfect**
S 3	ol	ola	olas	olsa
	Present Subjunctive	**Imperfect Subjunctive**	**Imperative**	**Present Participle**
S 3	ollo	olla		owth ola
				Past Participle

OMGUDHA (OMGUTH): to hide oneself				
	Present	**Imperfect**	**Preterite**	**Pluperfect**
S 3	omguth	omgudha	omgudhas	omguthsa
	Present Subjunctive	**Imperfect Subjunctive**	**Imperative**	**Present Participle**
S 3	omgutho	omgutha		owth omgudha
				Past Participle

N.B. Used with *rak*

OMLATH (OMLATH): to fight				
	Present	**Imperfect**	**Preterite**	**Pluperfect**
S 3	omlath	omladhy	omladhas	omlathsa
	Present Subjunctive	**Imperfect Subjunctive**	**Imperative**	**Present Participle**
S 3	omlatho	omlatha		owth omlath
				Past Participle
				omlathys

OMWOLGHY (OMWOLGH): to wash oneself, get washed				
	Present	**Imperfect**	**Preterite**	**Pluperfect**
S 3	omwolgh	omwolghy	omwolghas	omwolghsa
	Present Subjunctive	**Imperfect Subjunctive**	**Imperative**	**Present Participle**
S 3	omwolgho	omwolgha		owth omwolghy
				Past Participle

PARUSY(PARUS): to cook, prepare, make ready				
	Present	**Imperfect**	**Preterite**	**Pluperfect**
S 3	parus	parusy	parusas	parussa
	Present Subjunctive	**Imperfect Subjunctive**	**Imperative**	**Present Participle**
S 3	parusso	parussa		ow parusy
				Past Participle
				parusys

PE (PE): to pay				
	Present	**Imperfect**	**Preterite**	**Pluperfect**
S 3	pe	pe	pes	pesa
	Present Subjunctive	**Imperfect Subjunctive**	**Imperative**	**Present Participle**
S 2			pegh	ow pe
S 3	peo	pea		
				Past Participle
				pys

Example: *pe dhe* - to pay (someone) out, punish;
pys da - contented, delighted; *drok pys* - displeased, dissatisfied

PEDRY (PODER): to rot, decay				
	Present	**Imperfect**	**Preterite**	**Pluperfect**
S 1	podraf	pedryn	pedrys	potsen
S 2	pedryth	pedrys	petsys	potses
S 3	peder	pedry	podras	potsa
P 1	pedryn	pedryn	petsyn	potsen
P 2	pedrough	pedreugh	petsough	potseugh
P 3	pedrons	pedrens	potsons	potsens
	Present Subjunctive	**Imperfect Subjunctive**	**Imperative**	**Present Participle**
S 1	pedryf	podren		ow pedry
S 2	pedry	podres	poder	
S 3	pottro	podra	pedrens	**Past Participle**
P 1	pedryn	podren	pedryn	pedrys
P 2	pedrough	podreugh	pedreugh	
P 3	pottrons	podrens	pedrens	

PERTHY (PORTH): to bear, sustain, endure, withstand, suffer				
	Present	**Imperfect**	**Preterite**	**Pluperfect**
S 3	perth	perthy	porthas	porthsa
	Present Subjunctive	**Imperfect Subjunctive**	**Imperative**	**Present Participle**
S 2			porth	ow perthy
S 3	portho	portha		
				Past Participle
				perthys

Example: *perthy orth* - to hold out against, put up with
Takes some abstract nouns as object to mean "be affected by";
perthy avy orth - to bear malice against; *perthy awher* - to bear sorrow, worry; *na borth awher* - don't worry; *perthy cof* - to remember; *perthy danjer* - to hesitate; *perthy meth* - to bear shame ; *perthy own* - to dread

See also ***PARAGH*** in Defective Verbs, page 110

PESYA (PES): to last, continue				
	Present	**Imperfect**	**Preterite**	**Pluperfect**
S 3	pys	pesya	pesyas	pessa
	Present Subjunctive	**Imperfect Subjunctive**	**Imperative**	**Present Participle**
S 3	pesyo	pesya		ow pesya
				Past Participle
				pesyes

PEWY(PEW): to own, possess, win, be entitled to*					
	Present	**Imperfect**	**Preterite**	**Pluperfect**	**Habitual Imperf**
S 1	pewof	pewen	pewvef	pewvyen	pewvedhen
S 2	pewos	pewes	pewves	pewvyes	pewvedhes
S 3	pew	pewo	pewva	pewvya	pewvedha
P 1	pewon	pewen	pewven	pewvyen	pewvedhen
P 2	pewough	peweugh	pewveugh	pewvyeugh	pewvedheugh
P 3	pewons, pewyns	pewens	pewvons	pewvyens	pewvedhens
	Pres Subjunctive	**Imp Subjunctive**	**Future**	**Imperative**	**Present Participle**
S 1	pewfyf	pewfen	pewvydhaf		ow pew
S 2	pewfy	pewfes	pewvydhyth	pewvyth	
S 3	pewfo	pewfa	pewvyth	pewvedhens	**Past Participle**
P 1	pewfen, pewfon	pewfen	pewvydhyn	pewvedhen	pewvedhys
P 2	pewfeugh, pewfough	pewfeugh	pewvydhough	pewvedeugh	
P 3	pewfons	pewfens	pewvydhons	pewvedhens	

*Defective verb based on ***BOS***

PLEKYA (PLEK): to please				
	Present	**Imperfect**	**Preterite**	**Pluperfect**
S 3	plek	plekya	plekyas	pleksa
	Present Subjunctive	**Imperfect Subjunctive**	**Imperative**	**Present Participle**
S 3	plekyo	plekya		ow plekya
				Past Participle
				plekyes

N.B. Used with *dhe* + 2nd state mutation.

PONYA (PON): to run, trot				
	Present	**Imperfect**	**Preterite**	**Pluperfect**
S 1	ponyaf	ponyen	ponys	ponsen
S 2	ponyth	ponyes	ponsys	ponses
S 3	pon	ponya	ponyas	ponsa
P 1	ponyn	ponyen	ponsyn	ponsen
P 2	ponyough	ponyeugh	ponsough	ponseugh
P 3	ponyons	ponyens	ponsons	ponsens
0	ponyr	ponys	ponyas	ponsys
	Present Subjunctive	**Imperfect Subjunctive**	**Imperative**	**Present Participle**
S 1	ponyf	ponyen		ow ponya
S 2	pony	ponyes	pon	
S 3	ponyo	ponya	ponyens	**Past Participle**
P 1	ponyn	ponyen	ponyn	ponyes, ponyys
P 2	ponyough	ponyeugh	ponyeugh	
P 3	ponyons	ponyens	ponyens	
0	ponyer	ponys		

N.B. Used only with living creatures.
For water, roots, vehicles, and also living creatures use ***RESEK***

PREDERY (PREDER): to think, reflect, consider				
	Present	**Imperfect**	**Preterite**	**Pluperfect**
S 1			prederys	
S 3	preder	predery	prederys	predersa
	Present Subjunctive	**Imperfect Subjunctive**	**Imperative**	**Present Participle**
S 3	prederro	prederra		ow predery
				Past Participle
				prederys

N.B. Used with *a* + 2nd state mutation.

PRENA: to buy, redeem, pay for, merit – see page 8

PREVY (PROF): to prove, try, test				
	Present	**Imperfect**	**Preterite**	**Pluperfect**
S 1	provaf	prevyn	prevys	profsen
S 2	prevyth	prevys	prefsys	profses
S 3	pref	prevy	provas	profsa
P 1	prevyn	prevyn	prefsyn	profsen
P 2	prevough	preveugh	prefseugh	profseugh
P 3	prevons	prevens	profsons	profsens
	Present Subjunctive	**Imperfect Sujunctive**	**Imperative**	**Present Participle**
S 1	prevyf	proven		ow prevy
S 2	prevy	proves	prof	
S 3	proffo	prova	prevens	**Past Participle**
P 1	prevyn	proven	prevyn	prevys, preys
P 2	prevough	preveugh	preveugh	
P 3	proffons	provens	prevens	

PYSKESSA: to catch fish, go fishing.

N.B. *Pyskessa* is only used in the infinitive or present participle
ow pyskessa - fishing

For other similar verbs see page 106

PYSY (PYS) / PESY (PES)/ PEJY (PEJ): to pray, beg, entreat				
	Present	**Imperfect**	**Preterite**	**Pluperfect**
S 1	pysaf/pesaf/pejaf	pysyn/pesyn/pejyn	pysys/pesys/pejys	pyssen/pessyn
S 2	pysys/pesys/pejys	pysys/pesys/pejys	pyssys/pessys	pysses/pesses
S 3	pys/pes	pysy/pesy/pejy	pysys/pesys/pejys	pyssa/pessa
P 1	pysyn/pesyn/pejyn	pysyn/pesyn/pejyn	pyssyn/pessyn	pyssen/pessen
P 2	pysough/pesough/ pejough	pyseugh/peseugh/ pejeugh	pyssough/ pessough	pysseugh/ pesseugh
P 3	pysons/pesons/ pejons	pysens/pesens/ pejens	pyssons/pessons	pyssens/pessens
	Present Subjunctive	**Imperfect Subjunctive**	**Imperative**	**Present Participle**
S 1	pyssyf/pessyf	pyssen/pessen		ow pysy/ow pesy/ow pejy
S 2	pyssy/pessy	pysses/pesses	pys/pes/pej	
S 3	pysso/pesso	pyssa/pessa	pysens/pesens/ pejens	**Past Participle**
P 1	pyssyn/pessyn	pyssen/pessen	pysyn/pesyn/pejyn	pysys/pesys/ pejys
P 2	pysseugh/ pesseugh	pysseugh/ pesseugh	pyseugh/peseugh/ pejeugh	
P 3	pyssons/pessons	pyssens/pessens	pysens/pesens/ pejens	

N.B. Used with *a* + 2nd state mutation or *gans*
Example: *pysy gans* - to intercede for
There are no references in texts to double j – *"jj"*

RANNA (RAN): to divide, share, distribute				
	Present	**Imperfect**	**Preterite**	**Pluperfect**
S 3	ran	ranna	rannas	ransa
	Present Subjunctive	**Imperfect Subjunctive**	**Imperative**	**Present Participle**
S 3	ranno	ranna		ow ranna
				Past Participle
				rynnys

N.B. Used with *ynter*

REDYA (RED): to read ***Also SPEDYA (SPED): to succeed, progress, hasten***				
	Present	**Imperfect**	**Preterite**	**Pluperfect**
S 1	redyaf	redyen	redys	retsen
S 2	redyth	redyes	retsys	retses
S 3	red	redya	redyas	retsa
P 1	redyn	redyen	retsyn	retsen
P 2	redyough	redyeugh	retsough	retseugh
P 3	redyons	redyens	retsons	retsens
	Present Subjunctive	**Imperfect Subjunctive**	**Imperative**	**Present Participle**
S 1	redyf	redyen		ow redya
S 2	redy	redyes	red	
S 3	redyo	redya	redyens	**Past Participle**
P 1	redyn	redyen	redyn	redyes, redys
P 2	redyough	redyeugh	redyeugh	
P 3	redyons	redyens	redyens	

N.B. 1st person singular (S1) *SPEDYA - spet*
Example: *spedya negys* - to bring a matter to a successful conclusion

REVYA (REF): to row				
	Present	**Imperfect**	**Preterite**	**Pluperfect**
S 3	ref	revya	revyas	refsa
	Present Subjunctive	**Imperfect Subjunctive**	**Imperative**	**Present Participle**
S 3	reffo	reva		ow revya
				Past Participle
				revyes

RY (RO): to give, grant, deliver, bestow ***Also OMRY (OMRO): to surrender***				
	Present	**Imperfect**	**Preterite**	**Pluperfect**
S 1	rof	ren	res	rosen
S 2	reth	res	ressys	roses
S 3	re	ry	ros	rosa
P 1	ren	ren	resen	rosen
P 2	rough	reugh	resough	roseugh
P 3	rons	rens	rosons	rosens
0	rer	res	ros	rosys
	Present Subjunctive	**Imperfect Subjunctive**	**Imperative**	**Present Participle**
S 1	ryllyf	rollen		ow ry
S 2	rylly	rolles	ro, roy	
S 3	rollo	rolla	rens	**Past Participle**
P 1	ryllyn	rollen	ren	res
P 2	ryllough	rolleugh	reugh	
P 3	rollons	rollens	rens	

N.B. Used with *dhe* + 2nd state mutation
Example: *ro dhym dha dhorn* - give me your hand

SAWTHANAS (SAWTHAN): to surprise, startle				
	Present	**Imperfect**	**Preterite**	**Pluperfect**
S 3	sawthan	sawtheny	sawthenys	sawthensa
	Present Subjunctive	**Imperfect Subjunctive**	**Imperative**	**Present Participle**
S 3	sawthenno	sawthenna		ow sawthanas
				Past Participle
				sawthenys

SAWYA (SAW): to save, preserve, cure, heal				
	Present	**Imperfect**	**Preterite**	**Pluperfect**
S 3	saw	sawya	sawyas	sawsa
	Present Subjunctive	**Imperfect Subjunctive**	**Imperative**	**Present Participle**
S 3	sawo	sawa		ow sawya
				Past Participle
				sawyes

SCRYFA (SCRYF): to write				
	Present	**Imperfect**	**Preterite**	**Pluperfect**
S 3	scryf	scryfa	scryfas	scryfsa
	Present Subjunctive	**Imperfect Subjunctive**	**Imperative**	**Present Participle**
S 3	scryffo	scryffa		ow scryfa
				Past Participle
				scryfys

N.B. Used with *gans*
Example: *scryfys gans* - written by

SCUBA (SCUP): to sweep, brush				
	Present	**Imperfect**	**Preterite**	**Pluperfect**
S 1	scubaf	scuben	scubys	scupsen
S 2	scubyth	scubes	scupsys	scupses
S 3	scup	scuba	scubas	scupsa
P 1	scubyn	scuben	scupsyn	scupsen
P 2	scubough	scubeugh	scupsough	scupseugh
P 3	scubons	scubens	scupsons	scupsens
0	scubyr	scubas	scubys	scupsys
	Present Subjunctive	**Imperfect Subjunctive**	**Imperative**	**Present Participle**
S 1	scuppyf	scuppen		ow scuba
S 2	scuppy	scuppes	scup	
S 3	scuppo	scuppa	scubens	**Past Participle**
P 1	scuppyn	scuppen	scubyn	scubys
P 2	scuppough	scuppeugh	scubeugh	
P 3	scuppons	scuppens	scubens	
0	scupper	scuppys		

SCUSY (SCUS): to get away quickly, evade, take fright				
	Present	**Imperfect**	**Preterite**	**Pluperfect**
S 3	scus	scusy	scusas	scussa
	Present Subjunctive	**Imperfect Subjunctive**	**Imperative**	**Present Participle**
S 3	scusso	scussa		ow scusy
				Past Participle
				scusys

N.B. Used with *rak*

SEGHA (SEGH): to dry, wipe *Also DESEGHA: to dry up*				
	Present	**Imperfect**	**Preterite**	**Pluperfect**
S 2			syghsys	
S 3	segh	segha	seghas	seghsa
	Present Subjunctive	**Imperfect Subjunctive**	**Imperative**	**Present Participle**
S 3	segho	segha		ow segha
				Past Participle
				seghys, syghys

SERRY (SOR): to anger, offend, be angry				
	Present	**Imperfect**	**Preterite**	**Pluperfect**
S 3	ser	serry	sorras	sorsa
	Present Subjunctive	**Imperfect Subjunctive**	**Imperative**	**Present Participle**
S 2			sor	ow serry
S 3	sorro	sorra		
				Past Participle
				serrys

N.B. Used with *orth* + 2nd state mutation

SETTYA (SET): to set, put, place				
	Present	**Imperfect**	**Preterite**	**Pluperfect**
S 3	set	settya	settyas	setsa
	Present Subjunctive	**Imperfect Subjunctive**	**Imperative**	**Present Participle**
S 3	settyo	settya		ow settya
				Past Participle
				settyes, settys

Example: *settya orth/dhe/erbyn* - to oppose; *settya chy* - to let a house; *settya dalghen* - to lay hold of

SEVEL (SAF): to stand, rise, remain, desist				
	Present	**Imperfect**	**Preterite**	**Pluperfect**
S 1	savaf	sevyn	sevys	safsen
S 2	sevyth	sevys	sefsys	safses
S 3	sef	sevy	sevys, savas	safsa
P 1	sevyn	sevyn	sefsyn	safsen
P 2	sevough	seveugh	sefsough	safseugh
P 3	sevons	sevens	safsons	safsens
	Present Subjunctive	**Imperfect Subjunctive**	**Imperative**	**Present Participle**
S 1	saffyf	saffen, syffyf		ow sevel
S 2	saffy	saffes, syffy	saf, sa'	
S 3	saffo	saffa	sevens	**Past Participle**
P 1	saffyn	saffen	sevyn	sevys
P 2	saffough	saffeugh	seveugh	
P 3	saffons	saffens	sevens	

Example: *sevel orth* - to abstain from, resist; *saf yn-ban/sa'ban* - to rise up

SEWYA (SEW): to follow, result, pursue				
	Present	**Imperfect**	**Preterite**	**Pluperfect**
S 3	sew	sewya	sewyas	sewsa
	Present Subjunctive	**Imperfect Subjunctive**	**Imperative**	**Present Participle**
S 3	sewyo	sewya		ow sewya
				Past Participle
				sewyes

SHYNDYA (SHYND): to injure, ruin, disgrace				
	Present	**Imperfect**	**Preterite**	**Pluperfect**
S 3	shynd	shyndya	shyndyas	shyntsa
	Present Subjunctive	**Imperfect Subjunctive**	**Imperative**	**Present Participle**
S 3	shyndyo	shyndya		ow shyndya
				Past Participle
				shyndyes

SKETHRY (SKETHER): to prune, chop, splinter				
	Present	**Imperfect**	**Preterite**	**Pluperfect**
S 1	skethraf	skethryn	skethrys	skethsen
S 2	skethryth	skethrys	skethsys	skethses
S 3	skether	skethry	skethras	skethsa
P 1	skethryn	skethryn	skethsyn	skethsen
P 2	skethrough	skethreugh	skethsough	skethseugh
P 3	slethrons	skethrens	skethsons	skethsens
0	skethyr	skethrys	slethras	skethsys
	Present Subjunctive	**Imperfect Subjunctive**	**Imperative**	**Present Participle**
S 1	skethryf	skethren		ow skethry
S 2	skethry	skethres	skether	
S 3	skethro	skethra	skethrens	**Past Participle**
P 1	skethryn	skethren	skethryn	skethrys
P 2	skethrough	skethreugh	skethreugh	
P 3	skethrons	slethrens	skethrens	
0	skethrer	skethrys		

SONA (SON): to bless				
	Present	**Imperfect**	**Preterite**	**Pluperfect**
S 3	son	sona	sonas	sonsa
	Present Subjunctive	**Imperfect Subjunctive**	**Imperative**	**Present Participle**
S 3	sonno	sonna		ow sona
				Past Participle
				sonys

SPENA (SPEN): to spend, use up, expend (time and money)				
	Present	**Imperfect**	**Preterite**	**Pluperfect**
S 3	spen	spena	spenas	spensa
	Present Subjunctive	**Imperfect Subjunctive**	**Imperative**	**Present Participle**
S 3	speno	spena		ow spena
				Past Participle
				spenys

SPLANNA (SPLAN): to shine				
	Present	**Imperfect**	**Preterite**	**Pluperfect**
S 3	splan	splana	splanas	splansa
	Present Subjunctive	**Imperfect Subjunctive**	**Imperative**	**Present Participle**
S 3	splanno	splanna		ow splanna
				Past Participle
				splannys

SQUYCHYA (SQUYCH): to jerk, twitch				
	Present	**Imperfect**	**Preterite**	**Pluperfect**
S 3	squych	squychya	sqychyas	squychsa
	Present Subjunctive	**Imperfect Subjunctive**	**Imperative**	**Present Participle**
S 3	squychyo	squychya		ow squychya
				Past Participle
				squychyes

STANKYA (STANK): to trample heavily on				
	Present	**Imperfect**	**Preterite**	**Pluperfect**
S 3	stank	stankya	stankyas	stanksa
	Present Subjunctive	**Imperfect Subjunctive**	**Imperative**	**Present Participle**
S 3	stankyo	stankya		ow stankya
				Past Participle
				stankyes

SYLWEL (SYLW) / SELWEL (SALW): to save, be saved				
	Present	**Imperfect**	**Preterite**	**Pluperfect**
S.1	salwaf	sylwyn	sylwys	salwsen, sawlsen
S 2	sylwyth	sylwys	sylwsys	salwses, sawlses
S 3	sylow	sylwy	sylwys	salwsa, sawlsa
P 1	sylwyn	sylwyn	sylwsyn	salwsen, sawlsen
P 2	sylwough	sylweugh	sylwsough	salwseugh, sawlseugh
P 3	sylwons	sylwens	salwsons, sawlsons	salwsens, sawlsens
	Present Subjunctive	**Imperfect Subjunctive**	**Imperative**	**Present Participle**
S 1	sylwyf	salwen		ow sylwel
S 2	sylwy	salwes	sylw/salw	
S 3	salwo	salwa	sylwens	
P 1	sylwyn	salwen	sylwyn	
P 2	sylwough	salweugh	sylweugh	**Past Participle**
P 3	salwons	salwens	salwens	sylwys

N.B. Used with *dhe* + 2nd state mutation

SYNSY (SYNS) / SENSY (SENS): to hold, grasp, observe, value, feel, consider				
	Present	**Imperfect**	**Preterite**	**Pluperfect**
S 1	synsaf	synsyn	synsys	synssen
S 2	synsyth	synsys	synssys	synsses
S 3	syns	synsy	synsys	synssa
P 1	synsyn	synsyn	synssyn	synssen
P 2	synsough	synseugh	synssough	synsseugh
P 3	synsons	synsens	synssons	synssens
0	synsyr	synsys	synsys	synssys
	Present Subjunctive	**Imperfect Subjunctive**	**Imperative**	**Present Participle**
S 1	synsyf	synsen		ow synsy
S 2	synsy	synses	syns	
S 3	synso	synsa	synses, synsens	**Past Participle**
P 1	synsyn	synsen	synsyn	synsys
P 2	synseugh	synseugh	synseugh	
P 3	synsons	synsens	synsens	
0	synser	sysnses		

Example: *synsys dhe* - beholden to, under an obligation to;
synsy fer - to hold a fair

TARDHA (TARTH): to burst, explode, break forth				
	Present	**Imperfect**	**Preterite**	**Pluperfect**
S 3	tarth	tardha	tardhas	tarthsa
	Present Subjunctive	**Imperfect Subjunctive**	**Imperative**	**Present Participle**
S 3	tartho	tartha		ow tardha
				Past Participle
				tardhys

TAVA (TAF): to touch, stroke				
	Present	**Imperfect**	**Preterite**	**Pluperfect**
S 1	tavaf	taven	tevys	tafsen
S 2	tevyth	taves	tefsys	tafses
S 3	taf, tava	tava	tavas	tafsa
P 1	tevyn	taven	tefsyn	tafsen
P 2	tevough	taveugh	tefsough	tafseugh
P 3	tavons	tavens	tafsons	tafsens
0	tevyr	tevys	tavas	tefsys
	Present Subjunctive	**Imperfect Subjunctive**	**Imperative**	**Present Participle**
S 1	tyffyf	taffen		ow tava
S 2	tyffy	taffes	taf	
S 3	taffo	taffa	tavens	**Past Participle**
P 1	tyffyn	taffen	tevyn	tevys
P 2	tyffough	taffeugh	teveugh	
P 3	taffons	taffens	tavens	
0	taffer	tyffys		

TEMPRA (TEMPER): to tame, subdue, control				
	Present	**Imperfect**	**Preterite**	**Pluperfect**
S 3	temper	tempra	tempras	tempersa
	Present Subjunctive	**Imperfect Subjunctive**	**Imperative**	**Present Participle**
S 3	tempro	tempra	temper	ow tempra
				Past Participle
				temprys

TENNA (TEN): to pull, pluck				
	Present	**Imperfect**	**Preterite**	**Pluperfect**
S 3	ten	tenna	tennas	tensa
	Present Subjunctive	**Imperfect Subjunctive**	**Imperative**	**Present Participle**
S 3	tenno	tenna		ow tenna
				Past Participle
				tennys, tynnys

Example: *tenna dhe* - to shoot at

TERRY (TOR): to break, destroy, tear down				
	Present	**Imperfect**	**Preterite**	**Pluperfect**
S 3	ter	terry	torras	torsa
	Present Subjunctive	**Imperfect Subjunctive**	**Imperative**	**Present Participle**
S 2			tor	ow terry
S 3	torro	torra		
				Past Participle
				terrys

TERVY (TERF): to make a din				
	Present	**Imperfect**	**Preterite**	**Pluperfect**
S 3	terf	tervy	tervys	terfsa
	Present Subjunctive	**Imperfect Subjunctive**	**Imperative**	**Present Participle**
S 3	terfo	terfa		ow tervy
				Past Participle
				tervys

TEWEL (TAW): to be silent				
	Present	**Imperfect**	**Preterite**	**Pluperfect**
S 1	tawaf	tewyn	tewys	tawsen
S 2	tewyth	tewys	tewsys	tawses
S 3	tew	tewy	tewys	tawsa
P 1	tewyn	tewyn	tewsyn	tawsen
P 2	tewough	teweugh	tewsough	tawseugh
P 3	tewons	tewens	tawsons	tawsens
0	tewyr	tewys	tewys	tewsys
	Present Subjunctive	**Imperfect Subjunctive**	**Imperative**	**Present Participle**
S 1	tewyf	tawen		ow tewel
S 2	tewy	tawes	taw	
S 3	tawo	tawa	tewens	**Past Participle**
P 1	tewyn	tawen	tewyn	tewys
P 2	tewough	taweugh	teweugh	
P 3	tawons	tawens	tewens	
0	tewer	tewsys		

TEWLEL (TOWL): to throw, cast, contrive, intend				
	Present	**Imperfect**	**Preterite**	**Pluperfect**
S 3	tewl	tewly	tewlys	towlsa
	Present Subjunctive	**Imperfect Subjunctive**	**Imperative**	**Present Participle**
S 2			towl	ow tewlel
S 3	towlo	towla		
				Past Participle
				tewlys

Example: *tewlel ros* - to shoot a net; *tewlel towl* - to make a plan; *tewlel paw* - to set foot; *tewlel deudhorn war* - to lay hands on early/roughly

TONTYA (TONT): to be cheeky				
	Present	**Imperfect**	**Preterite**	**Pluperfect**
S 3	tont	tontya	tontyas	tontsa
	Present Subjunctive	**Imperfect Subjunctive**	**Imperative**	**Present Participle**
S 3	tontyo	tontya		ow tontya
				Past Participle
				tontyes

TRELYA (TREL): to turn, twist, translate				
	Present	**Imperfect**	**Preterite**	**Pluperfect**
S 3	trel	trelya	trelyas	trelsa
	Present Subjunctive	**Imperfect Subjunctive**	**Imperative**	**Present Participle**
S 3	trelyo	trelya		ow trelya
				Past Participle
				trelyes

Example: *trelya dhe ves* - turn away; *trelya yn mes a* - pervert; *trelya adro dhe* - wind round; *trelya wor'tu ma* - turn this way

TREMENA (TREMEN): to pass, cross, elapse, pass away, exceed Also CAMDREMENA (CAMDREMEN): to trespass				
	Present	**Imperfect**	**Preterite**	**Pluperfect**
S 3	tremen	tremena	tremenas	tremensa
	Present Subjunctive	**Imperfect Subjunctive**	**Imperative**	**Present Participle**
S 3	tremenno	tremenna		ow tremena
				Past Participle
				tremenys

TROYLLYA (TROYLL): to twist, whirl, turn on a lathe				
	Present	**Imperfect**	**Preterite**	**Pluperfect**
S 3	troyll	troyllya	troyllyas	troyllsa
	Present Subjunctive	**Imperfect Subjunctive**	**Imperative**	**Present Participle**
S 3	troyllyo	troyllya		ow troyllya
				Past Participle
				troyllyes

N.B. *pollen troyllya* - whirlpool

TRYGA (TRYK): to stay, abide, inhabit, settle, remain, dwell				
	Present	**Imperfect**	**Preterite**	**Pluperfect**
S 3	tryk, tryg	tryga	trygas	tryksa
	Present Subjunctive	**Imperfect Subjunctive**	**Imperative**	**Present Participle**
S 3	trycco	trycca		ow tryga
				Past Participle
				trygys

TRYGHY (TRYGH): to conquer, be victorious				
	Present	**Imperfect**	**Preterite**	**Pluperfect**
S 3	trygh	tryghy	tryghas	tryghsa
	Present Subjunctive	**Imperfect Subjunctive**	**Imperative**	**Present Participle**
S 3	trygho	trygha		ow tryghy
				Past Participle
				tryghys

TY (TY): to swear				
	Present	**Imperfect**	**Preterite**	**Pluperfect**
S 1	tof	ten	tes	tosen
S 2	teth	tes	tessys	toses
S 3	te	te	tos	tosa
P 1	ten	ten	tesen	tosen
P 2	tough	teugh	tesough	toseugh
P 3	tons	tens	tesons	tosens
0	ter	tes	tos	tosys
	Present Subjunctive	**Imperfect Subjunctive**	**Imperative**	**Present Participle**
S 1	tyllyf	tollen		ow ty
S 2	tylly	tolles	to	
S 3	tollo	tolla	tens	**Past Participle**
P 1	tyllyn	tollen	ten	tes
P 2	tyllough	tolleugh	teugh	
P 3	tollons	tollens	tens	
0	toller	tollys		

N.B. Do not confuse with ***TY* : to roof, cover from rain, slate, lay tiles**

TYLLY (TAL): to pay, owe, be worth, deserve
Also ATTYLLY (ATAL): to repay

	Present	**Imperfect**	**Preterite**	**Pluperfect**
S 1	talaf	tellen	tylys	talvyen
S 2	tylyth	telles	tylsys	talvyes
S 3	tal	tella	tylys	talvya
P 1	tylyn	tellen	tylsyn	talvyen
P 2	tylough	telleugh	tylsough	talvyeugh
P 3	talons	tellens	talsons	talvyens
0	tyllyr	telles	tylys	talvyes

	Present Subjunctive	**Imperfect Subjunctive**	**Future**	**Imperative**	**Present Participle**
S 1	tyllyf	talfen	talvydhaf		ow tylly
S 2	tylly	talfes	talvydhyth	tal	
S 3	tallo	talfa	talvyth	telens	**Past Participle**
P 1	tyllyn	talfen	talvydhyn	telen	tylys/ *talvedhys, talvys
P 2	tyllough	talfeugh	talvydhough	teleugh	
P 3	tallons	talfens	talvydhons	telens	
0	taller	talfes	talvydher		

N.B.** An alternative infinitive or verbal noun ***TALVOS is sometimes used with Past Participle *talvedhys* or *talvys* to mean “to value, price”.
In Pluperfect / Conditional tense *my a dalvya* – I should have, ought to have
Otherwise conjugations are the same as ***TYLLY.***
N.B. Use ***TYLLY*** **-** to pay
Example: *my a vyn tylly an reken* - I will pay the bill
N.B. Use ***PRENA*** **-** to pay for
Example: *my a vyn prena an dewas* - I will pay for the drink
N.B. To avoid confusion with ***TYLLY:*** **to owe, pay**
and ***TELLY:*** **to drill, bore a hole through**
the subjunctive might be formed with auxiliary verbs
rather than in imitation of *RY*

USYA (US): to use, be accustomed to, habitually wear, take to eat or drink, perform				
	Present	**Imperfect**	**Preterite**	**Pluperfect**
S 3	us	usya	usyas	ussa
	Present Subjunctive	**Imperfect Subjunctive**	**Imperative**	**Present Participle**
S 3	usso	ussa		owth usya
				Past Participle
				usyes

VYAJYA (VYAJ): to travel				
	Present	**Imperfect**	**Preterite**	**Pluperfect**
S 3	vyaj	vyajya	vyajyas	vyachsa
	Present Subjunctive	**Imperfect Subjunctive**	**Imperative**	**Present Participle**
S 3	vyajyo	vyajya		ow vyajya
				Past Participle
				vyajyes

WHARFOS: to happen, befall				
	Present	**Imperfect**	**Preterite**	**Pluperfect**
S 3	wher	wharfya	wharfe	wharsa
	Present Subjunctive	**Imperfect Subjunctive**	**Future**	**Present Participle**
S 3	wharfo	wharfa	whyrfyth	ow wharfos
				Past Participle
				wharfedhys

N.B ***WHARFOS*** is a *BOS* compound found only in the 3rd person in tenses where *BOS* begins with a *b*. **Example**: *Pandr'a wher?* - what's happening? (Do not confuse with Defective verb ***WHER*: ails, distresses, pains** - see page 111).

Also ***DARFOS: to happen -*** a compound of *BOS* used only in Preterite and Past Participle which behaves in a similar way to *WHARFOS* where it is restricted to the forms where *BOS* begins with a *b*.

WHERTHYN (WHARTH): to laugh ***Also MYNWHERTHYN: to smile***				
	Present	**Imperfect**	**Preterite**	**Pluperfect**
S 3	wharth	wherthy	wharthas	wharthsa
	Present Subjunctive	**Imperfect Subjunctive**	**Imperative**	**Present Participle**
S 3	whartho	whartha		ow wherthyn
				Past Participle

WHETHA (WHETH): to blow, breathe				
	Present	**Imperfect**	**Preterite**	**Pluperfect**
S 3	wheth	whetha	whethas	whethsa
	Present Subjunctive	**Imperfect Subjunctive**	**Imperative**	**Present Participle**
S 3	whetho	whetha		ow whetha
				Past Participle
				whethys

WHYLAS (WHYLA): to seek, search for, examine				
	Present	**Imperfect**	**Preterite**	**Pluperfect**
S 3	whyla	whyly	whylys	whylsa
	Present Subjunctive	**Imperfect Subjunctive**	**Imperative**	**Present Participle**
S 2			whyla	ow whylas
S 3	whyllo	whylla		
				Past Participle
				whylys

YGERY (YGOR): to open, disclose				
	Present	**Imperfect**	**Preterite**	**Pluperfect**
S 1	ygeraf	ygeryn	ygerys	ygorsen
S 2	ygeryth	ygerys	ygersys	ygorses
S 3	ygor	ygery	ygoras	ygorsa
P 1	ygeryn	ygeryn	ygersyn	ygorsen
P 2	ygerough	ygereugh	ygersough	ygorseugh
P 3	ygerons	ygerens	ygorsons	ygorsens
0	ygeryr	ygerys	ygoras	ygorsys
	Present Subjunctive	**Imperfect Subjunctive**	**Imperative**	**Present Participle**
S 1	ygerryf	ygorren		owth ygery
S 2	ygerry	ygorres	ygor	
S 3	ygorro	ygorra	ygerens	**Past Participle**
P 1	ygerryn	ygorren	ygeryn	ygerys
P 2	ygerrough	ygorreugh	ygereugh	
P 3	ygorrons	ygorrens	ygerens	
0	ygerrer	ygorrys		

YNNYA (YNNY): to urge, incite				
	Present	**Imperfect**	**Preterite**	**Pluperfect**
S 3	ynny	ynnya	ynnyas	ynnysa
	Present Subjunctive	**Imperfect Subjunctive**	**Imperative**	**Present Participle**
S 2			ynny	owth ynnya
S 3	ynnyo	ynnya		
				Past Participle
				ynnyes

Example: *ynny war* - to press on

YSKYNNA (YSKYN): to ascend, climb, mount				
	Present	**Imperfect**	**Preterite**	**Pluperfect**
S 3	yskyn	yskynna	yskynnas	yskynsa
	Present Subjunctive	**Imperfect Subjunctive**	**Imperative**	**Present Participle**
S 3	yskynno	yskynna		owth yskynna
				Past Participle
				yskynnys

YSTYNNA (YSTYN): to reach, stretch out, extend, set sail				
	Present	**Imperfect**	**Preterite**	**Pluperfect**
S 3	ystyn	ystynna	ystynnas	ystynsa
	Present Subjunctive	**Imperfect Subjunctive**	**Imperative**	**Present Participle**
S 2			ystyn	
S 3	ystynno	ystynna		owth ystynna
				Past Participle
				ystynnys

VERBS USED ONLY IN THE INFINITIVE OR AS VERBAL NOUNS

All these verbs express gathering, hunting, collecting, chasing or catching

CONYNESSA	to go rabbiting, hunt rabbits
CREGYNNA	to gather shells
CUNYSSA	to gather fuel
DEVYSA	to hunt or worry sheep
GODHESSA	to catch moles
GODRA	to milk
GWYBESSA	to waste time (literally to catch gnats)
KEVELECCA	to catch woodcock
LEGESSA	to catch mice
MELA	to search for or gather honey
MELWHESSA	to collect snails
MESCLA	to hunt for mussels
MESSA	to gather acorns
MEYLESSA	to catch mullet
MORA	to gather blackberries
MYRGHESA	to chase after girls
PRENASSA	to go shopping
PRYVESSA	to hunt vermin
PYSKESSA	to go fishing
SYVYA	to gather strawberries
WHYLESSA	to hunt beetles
YDHNA	to hunt birds, go fowling

VERBS CONSTRUCTED FROM AN ADJECTIVE PLUS THE *–HE* SUFFIX OR SYLLABLE

Adding the *-HE* syllable as a suffix to an adjective creates a verb meaning "to make or enable",
i.e. *BER* (short) + *HE* = *BERHE* : *to shorten*
All such verbs follow the pattern for ***BERHE*** – see page 17

There are several examples in the main listings or paradigms including

BERHE:	***to shorten* (see page 17)**
GLANHE:	***to make clean* (see page 49)**
NESHE:	***to bring nearer* (see page 75)**

and further examples from the Nance dictionary are shown below, but you can also construct your own.

BEWHE	to enliven , quicken
BLOGHE	to make, become bald
CLERHE	to clear, brighten
COSELHE	to quieten, pacify
COTHHE	to grow old
CREFHE	to make strong, strengthen, grow stronger
DOFHE	to tame
DUHE	to blacken
FASTHE	to make firm, confirm
GWAKHE	to empty
GWANHE	to weaken
GWELLHE	to make better, improve, amend, speed
GWETHHE	to make worse, damage, deteriorate
GWETHYNHE	to toughen, make supple
GWYNHE	to whiten
HYRHE	to lengthen
KEHAVALHE	to compare, liken
LOMHE	to make bare, strip
LOWENHE	to make happy, rejoice, make glad
MEDHELHE	to soften
MOLHE	to make or become bold
MURHE	to magnify, make great
NOWETHHE	to renovate

OWNEKHE	to frighten
SCAFHE	to lighten, make quicker
SEMPELHE	to simplify
SPANHE/SPAVENHE	to quieten, lull (of weather)
SPLANHE	to make bright or clear
TANOWHE	to attenuate, make weaker, slim, scarce, reduce value
TEKHE	to beautify
TEWHE	to thicken, fatten
TEWLHE	to darken
TOMHE	to make hot (also *TOMMA* – to heat, warm)
TRENKHE	to make or become sour
TRYSTHE	to sadden
TYNHE	to tighten
UGHELHE	to exalt, heighten
WHARHE	to make gentler, civilize, humanize, make placid
YAGHE	to cure, make or become well, recover
YOWYNKHE	to make young, rejuvenate
YSELHE	to lower, degrade, diminish

DEFECTIVE VERBS

These verbs are restricted to just a few tenses or persons or are found in compound verbs;

BERN: concern, matter

Used only in 3rd person singular Present Future and often in the negative,

ny vern – no matter (it doesn't matter)
ny vern govyn orty – there's no harm in asking her
travyth ny vern – it doesn't matter at all
ny vern genef – I am not concerned

COTH/DEGOTH: be suitable, fitting, due, "falls to"

Degoth with the *DE-* prefix (2nd state mutation) is the strengthened form and intensifies the verb to which it is prefixed. Used only in 3rd person singular forms, used with *dhe* with or without combined pronouns. Forms other than Present Future are formed by adding the relevant endings from *BOS.*

y coth dhodho prena an dewosow –
it falls to him to buy the drinks (he must buy the drinks)
y tegothfya dhym –
it would be fitting for me (I ought)(Pluperfect/Conditional)
y coth dheugh bos war –
you ought to be careful
redya hy lyther a goth dh'y thas –
it is fitting for her father to read her letter

DELETH: be right, proper

Used only in 3rd person singular Present Future.

y teleth agan bos warbarth –
it's right that we (should)be together
a dheleth dhedha y wul? –
is it right that they do it?
y teleth Jowan prena car noweth rak an tylu –
it's right for John to buy a new car for the family
y teleth hy vos lowen hedhyu – it's right that she (should) be happy today

DUR: concerns, matters, is of interest

Used only in 3rd person singular Present Future and with infixed pronouns, (*'th* takes 5th state mutation)

ny'm dur – I am not concerned

clew, mara'th tur – listen, if it matters to you

anodho travyth ny's dur – she's not interested in it at all

MEDHES: speak, say

Used only in direct speech in verbal noun, 3rd person singular and 3rd person plural Present Future and occasionally 1st person singular. Used with *yn* as a particle and in the same form to represent present and past narration.

yn meth hy – she says/said

"ke dhe ves!" yn medhans y – "Go away!" they said

"my a vyn mos genough" yn medhaf – "I will go with you", I said

"ass yu drok an gewer!" yn meth Marya –"how bad the weather is!" said Mary

medhaf vy – I say...

PARAGH: endure, put up with, hold out, last

Verbal noun used only in compound sentences with auxiliary verbs *GALLOS* or *MYNNES*

ny vynnaf paragh henna – I won't put up with that

ny a yl paragh an howl oll an jeth – we can endure the sun all day

mar kylta paragh bys avorow – if you can hold out until tomorrow

RES: it is necessary

Rarely a verb, more often an adjective. Used only in 3rd person singular Present Future. Used with *dhe* with and without combined pronouns,

mar dha del res – as good as need be

ny res dhys – you need not

henna a res – that is necessary

ny res henna – that is not necessary

(Do not confuse with adjectival forms used with *BOS + dhe* , ***res yu dhym*** – I must (it is necessary to me), ***res vyth dhodho*** – he will have to

TAN: take! have!

Used only in 2nd person singular and 2nd person plural Imperative.

tan y lemmyn! **–** take them now!

tan dewas genef! **–** have a drink with me!

tan dha dywla mes a'th pokettys! **–** take your hands out of your pockets!

tanneugh agas cota kens mos! **–** take your coat before you go!

SKYLA: causes, there is cause or reason

Used only in 3rd person singular Present Future and without particles

devar skyla my dhe wul yndelma **–** duty causes me to act in this way

dhe voy skyla **–** all the more reason

hemma skyla an ergh dhe dedha **–** this causes the snow to melt

WAR: beware, mind, take care

Used only in 2nd person singular and 2nd person plural Imperative. Often used with *BOS.*

byth war – take care, be careful

wareugh an forth - mind the road

WHELES: turn

Used only in compounds such as

dewheles: return, come back

omwheles: fall down, overturn

domhel: overthrow, upset, subvert, ruin

WHER: it ails, pains, distresses

pandr'a wher dhys? **–** what distresses you?

(Do not confuse with abstract noun *AWHER* which is used with the verb *PERTHY:* to carry, bear, endure, i.e. *na borth awher* – don't worry, or with compound verb *WHARFOS* **– see page 102)**

SOME UNEXPECTED 2nd PERSON SINGULAR (S 2) IMPERATIVES

BEDHA (to dare)	***beth***
DARWAR (to be forewarned)	***def***
DEDHEWY (to promise)	***dedhow***
*(*N.B *dedhow* is also S3 Pres Fut "to lay eggs"!)	
DELYFRA (to release, set free)	***delyrf/delyr'vy***
DERYVAS (to declare, report)	***deryf*** **(see page 30)**
GORMEL (to praise)	***gormol***
GRAVYA (to carve)	***graf***
GROWEDHA (to lie down)	***groweth***
HALYA (to heave, haul)	***hala***
LESKY (to burn)	***losk***
MEDRA (to take aim)	***meder***
MEGY (to quell, extinguish, smoke)	***mok***
MERKYA (to mark, notice)	***mark***
PESKY (to feed, graze)	***pask***
POWES (to rest, halt)	***powes***
REGY (to tear)	***rok***
SENY (to sound, ring)	***son***
TELLY (to bore)	***toll***
TERRY (to break)	***tor*** **(see page 96)**
TREGHY (to cut)	***trogh***
WHYTHRA (to observe, look at)	***whythyr***

INDEX and page number

cultivate	*gonys*, 50
curb	*frona*, 44
cure	*sawya*, 86, *yaghe* (see *berhe*, 17)
damage	*gwethhe* (see *berhe*, 17)
dance	*donsya*, 34
darken	*tewlhe* (see *berhe*, 17)
decay	*pedry*, 79
decide	*ervyra*, 42
declare	*deryvas*, 31
defy	*defya* (see *fya*, 45)
degrade	*yselhe* (see *berhe*, 17)
delay	*gortos*, 52, *tarya* (see *fya*, 45)
deliver	*ry*, 85
deny	*nagha*, 74
descend	*dyeskynna*, 37
describe	*descryfa*, 30
deserve	*tylly*, 101
destroy	*terry*, 96
deteriorate	*gwethhe* (see *berhe*, 17)
die	*merwel* (see *gelwel*, 48)
diminish	*yselhe* (see *berhe*, 17)
din, to make a	*tervy*, 96
direct	*dysky*, 39, *lewyas*, 72
discharge	*dyllo*, 38
disclose	*ygery*, 104
discover	*cafos*, 19
disgrace	*shyndya*, 90
distress	*wher* (see Defective verbs, 111)
distribute	*ranna*, 83
divide	*ranna*, 83
do	*gul*, 12
double	*dobla*, 33
draw near	*nessa*, 75
drink	*eva*, 43
drip	*devera*, 31
drive	*lewyas*, 72
drown	*budhy*, 18
dry	*segha*, 88
dry up	*desegha* (see *segha*, 88)
dwell	*tryga*, 99

eat	*dybry,* 36
economise	*erbysy,* 42
educate	*dysky,* 39
elapse	*tremena,* 98
empty	*gwakhe* (see *berhe,* 17)
enchant	*huda,* 63
end	*dewedha,* 32
endure	*perthy,* 79, *paragh* (see Defective verbs, 110)
enliven	*bewhe* (see *berhe,* 17)
enter	*entra,* 41
entitled to, to be	*pewy,* 80
entrust	*commendya,* 24
equip	*darbary,* 29
err in thought	*camdyby,* 20
evade	*scusy,* 87
exaggerate	*gorlywa,* 51
exalt	*ughelhe* (see *berhe,* 17)
examine	*whylas,* 103
exceed	*tremena,* 98
exist	*bos,* 10
expect	*gwaytya,* 55
expire	*merwel* (see *gelwel,* 48)
explode	*tardha,* 94
extend	*hedhes,* 61, *ystynna,* 105
fail	*fyllel,* 46
fall	*codha,* 23
fatten	*tewhe* (see *berhe,* 17)
feel	*synsy,* 94
feel sensation	*clewes,* 23
fetch	*hedhes,* 60
fight	*omlath,* 77
fill	*lenwel,* 70
find	*cafos,* 19
finish	*dewedha,* 32
finish completely	*cowlwul,* 25
firm, to make	*fasthe* (see *berhe,* 17)
fish	*pyskessa* (see page 82, 106)
fit	*ewna,* 43
fitting, to be	*coth, degoth* (for both see Defective verbs, 109)
flee	*fya,* 45, *gwevya,* 57

pass away	*tremena,* 98
pay	*pe,* 78, *tylly,* 101
pay attention	*goslowes,* 53
pay for	*prena,* 8
perform	*usya,* 102
permit	*gasa,* 47
persuade	*dry,* 36
perturb	*amuvya* (see *muvya,* 73)
place	*gorra,* 51, *settya,* 88
placid, to make	*wharhe* (see *berhe,* 17)
play	*gwary,* 54
please	*plekya,* 81
pledge	*gwystla,* 59
pluck	*tenna,* 96
point out	*meneges,* 73
possess	*pewy,* 80
pour	*devera,* 32
pray	*pysy,* 83
prepare	*darbary,* 29, *parusy,* 78
preserve	*sawya,* 86
presume	*desevos,* 31
prevent	*lesta,* 71
progress	*spedya* (see *redya,* 84)
prohibit	*dyfen,* 37
proper, to be	*deleth* (see Defective verbs, 109)
propose	*muvya,* 73
protect	*gwytha,* 59
prove	*prevy,* 82
provide	*darbary,* 29, *dyghtya,* 38
prune	*skethry,* 90
publish	*dyllo,* 38
pull	*tenna,* 96
pursue	*sewya,* 89
push	*herdhya,* 62
put	*gorra,* 51, *settya,* 88
put to sea	*mora,* 73
put up with	*paragh* (see Defective verbs, 110)
quicken	*bewhe* (see *berhe,* 17)
quicker, to make	*scafhe* (see *berhe,* 17)
quieten	*coselhe, spanhe, spavenhe* (see *berhe,* 17)

raise	*drehevel,* 35
ram	*herdhya,* 62
reach	*hedhes,* 60, *ystynna,* 105
reach completely	*drehedhes,* 35
read	*redya,* 84
ready, to make	*parusy,* 78
reap	*myjy,* 74
reason, to have	*skyla* (see Defective verbs, 111)
rebuke	*keredhy,* 66
receive	*degemeres,* 30, *kemeres,* 65
recognise	*aswon,* 16
recount	*deryva,* 31
recover	*yaghe* (see *berhe,* 17)
redeem	*prena,* 8
refuse	*nagha,* 74
rejoice	*lowenhe* (see *berhe,* 17)
rejuvenate	*yowynkhe* (see *berhe,* 17)
relate	*leverel,* 71
relish	*blasa,* 18
remain	*sevel,* 89, *tryga,* 99
remove	*remuvya* (see *muvya,* 73)
renovate	*nowethhe* (see *berhe,* 17)
repay	*attylly* (see *tylly,* 101)
repent	*ola,* 77
replenish	*lenwel,* 70
reply	*gortheby,* 52
report	*meneges,* 73
restrain	*frona,* 44
result	*sewya,* 89
retaliate	*gortheby,* 52
return	*dewheles,* 32
right, to make	*ewna,* 43
rise	*sevel,* 89
rise (tide)	*morlenwel* (see *lenwel,* 70)
rob	*ladra,* 68
rot	*pedry,* 79
row	*revya,* 84
ruin	*shyndya,* 90
run	*ponya*, 81 (see also *fya,* 45)
sadden	*trysthe* (see *berhe,* 17)

sail	*golya*, 50, *mora*, 73
satisfy	*collenwel* (see *lenwel*, 70)
save, be saved	*sylwel*, 93
save (economise)	*erbysy*, 42
save (preserve)	*sawya*, 86
savour	*blasa*, 18
say	*leverel*, 71, *medhes* (see Defective verbs, 110)
scarce, to make	*tanowhe* (see *berhe*, 17)
search for	*whylas*, 103
see	*gweles*, 56
seek	*whylas*, 103
seize	*degemeres*, 30
sell	*gwertha*, 57
send	*danvon*, 29
send forth	*dyllo*, 38
serve	*dyghtya*, 38
set	*gorra*, 51, *settya*, 88
set free	*dyllo*, 38
set off (a gun)	*dyllo*, 38
set sail	*ystynna*, 105
settle	*tryga*, 99
sexual intercourse(have)	*kygya*, 67
share	*ranna*, 83
shed	*devera*, 32
shine	*splanna*, 91
shorten	*berhe*, 17
shout	*garma*, 46
show	*dysquedhes*, 40
shower	*devera*, 32
shut	*degea*, 30
sigh	*hanaja*, 60
silent, to be	*tewel*, 97
simplify	*sempelhe* (see *berhe*, 17)
sing	*cana*, 21
sit	*esedha*, 43
sleep	*cusca*, 28
slim, to make	*tanowhe* (see *berhe*, 17)
smell	*clewes*, 23
smile	*mynwherthyn* (see *wherthyn*, 103)
snap	*crakkya*, 25

soften	*medhelhe* (see *berhe,* 17)
sour, to make, become	*trenkhe* (see *berhe,* 17)
speak	*kewsel,* 67, *medhes* (see Defective verbs, 110)
speed	*gwellhe* (see *berhe,* 17)
spend	*spena,* 91
spike	*kentra,* 65
splinter	*skethry,* 90
stand	*sevel,* 89
stand by	*mentena,* 72
startle	*amuvya* (see *muvya,* 73), *sawthanas,* 85
state	*deryvas,* 31
stay	*tryga,* 99
steal	*ladra,* 68
steer	*lewyas,* 72
stick	*glena,* 49
stick fast	*kygya,* 67
stir	*gwaya,* 55, *muvya,* 73
stop (cease)	*hedhy,* 61
stop (wait)	*gortos,* 52
strengthen	*crefhe* (see *berhe,* 17)
stretch out	*ystynna,* 105
stride	*lamma,* 68, *lemmel,* 69
strike	*gweskel,* 57
strip	*lomhe* (see *berhe,* 17)
stroke	*tava,* 95
subdue	*tempra,* 95
submit	*obaya,* 76
succeed	*spedya* (see *redya,* 84)
suffer	*perthy,* 79, (see also *paragh* Defective verbs, 110)
suitable, to be	*coth, degoth* (for both see Defective verbs, 109)
supple, to make	*gwethynhe* (see *berhe,* 17)
supply	*darbary,* 29, *provya* (see *fya,* 45)
surprise	*sawthanas,* 85
surrender	*obaya,* 76, *omry* (see *ry,* 85)
sustain	*perthy,* 79
swallow	*lenky,* 69
swathe	*maylya,* 72
swear	*ty,* 100
sweep	*scuba,* 87
swim	*nyja,* 76, *nyjya,* 76

NOTES / *NOTENNOW*

NOTES / *NOTENNOW*

NOTES / *NOTENNOW*

NOTES / *NOTENNOW*

www.ingramcontent.com/pod-product-compliance
Ingram Content Group UK Ltd.
Pitfield, Milton Keynes, MK11 3LW, UK
UKHW041939190726
13854UKWH00004B/1681